50quickideas.com

FIFTY
Quick
IDEAS
TO IMPROVE YOUR
TESTS

by

Gojko Adzic,

David Evans and **Tom Roden**

FIFTY QUICK IDEAS

TO IMPROVE YOUR TESTS

PRINT ISBN: **978-0-9930881-1-7**

Published on: 15 May 2015
Copyright © Neuri Consulting LLP
Authors: Gojko Adzic, David Evans and Tom Roden
Copy-editor: Marjory Bisset
Design and layout: Nikola Korac

Published by:
Neuri Consulting LLP
25 Southampton Buildings
London WC2A2AL
United Kingdom

CONTENTS

INTRODUCTION

This book will help you test your software better, easier and faster. It's a collection of ideas we've used with various clients in many different contexts, from small web start-ups to the world's largest banks, to help team members collaborate better on defining and executing tests. Many of these ideas also help teams engage their business stakeholders better in defining key expectations and improve the quality of their software products.

Who is this book for?

This book is aimed at cross-functional teams working in an iterative delivery environment, planning with user stories and testing frequently changing software under the tough time pressure of short iterations. The intended audience are people with a solid understanding of the basics of software testing, who are looking for ideas on how to improve their tests and testing-related activities. The ideas in this book will be useful to many different roles, including testers, analysts and developers. You will find plenty of tips on how to organise your work better so that it fits into short iterative cycles or flow-based processes, and how to help your team define and organise testing activities better.

Who is this book not for?

This book doesn't cover the basics of software testing, nor does it try to present a complete taxonomy of all the activities a team needs to perform to inspect and improve the quality of their software. It's a book about improving testing activities, not setting up the basics. We assume that readers know about exploratory testing and test automation, the difference between unit tests and integration tests, and the key approaches to defining tests. In short, this isn't the first book about testing you should read. There are plenty of good basic books out there, so read them first and then come back. Please don't hate us because we skipped the basics, but there is only so much space in the book and other people cover the basics well enough already.

What's inside?

Unsurprisingly, the book contains exactly fifty ideas. They are grouped into four major parts:

- *Generating testing ideas*: This part deals with activities for teams to engage stakeholders in more productive discussions around needs and expectations. The ideas in this part are equally applicable to manual and automated testing, and should be particularly useful to people looking for inspiration on improving exploratory testing activities.
- *Designing good checks*: This part deals with defining good deterministic checks that can be easily automated. The ideas in this part will help you select better examples for your tests and specifications, and in particular help with the given-when-then style of acceptance criteria.
- *Improving testability*: This part contains useful architectural and modelling tricks for making software easier to observe and control, improve the reliability of testing systems and make test automation code easier to manage. It should be particularly useful for teams that suffer from unreliable automated tests due to complex architectural constraints.

• *Managing large test suites*: This part provides tips and suggestions on dealing with the long-term consequences of iterative delivery. In it, you'll find ideas on how to organise large groups of test cases so that they are easy to manage and update, and how to improve the structure of individual tests to simplify maintenance and reduce the costs associated with keeping your tests in sync with the frequently changing underlying software.

Each part contains ideas that we've used with teams over the last six to seven years to help them manage testing activities better. Software delivery is incredibly contextual, so some of our proposals will apply to your situation, and some won't. Treat all the ideas in this book as experiments.

Where to find more ideas?

There is only so much space in a book, and some of the ideas described deserve entire books of their own. We provide plenty of references for further study and pointers for more detailed research in the bibliography at the end of this book. If you're reading this book in electronic form, all the related books and articles are clickable links. If you're reading the book on paper, tapping the text won't help. To save you from having to type in long hyperlinks, we provide all the references online at *50quickideas.com*.

This book is part of a series of books on improving various aspects of iterative delivery. If you like it, check out the other books from the series at *50quickideas.com*.

FIFTY
Quick
IDEAS

GENERATING TEST IDEAS

DEFINE A SHARED BIG-PICTURE VIEW OF QUALITY

Quality is a notoriously difficult concept to pin down. Users mostly look at externally observable attributes, such as speed and usability. Business stakeholders look at financial performance. Developers mostly care about internal code structure. Testers sit somewhere between and try to connect all the dots. So many different levels of quality, and so many different perspectives, often lead to disagreements. A user might consider something a bug, but developers might classify it as an improvement request. Something one person considers critical might not even register on the scale of importance for someone from a different group. That is why a seemingly critical defect can be left in a software product for months, sitting in a bug tracking tool often serving just to prevent people sending more notifications about the same issue. This is also why software can be released to customers even when people on the delivery team know it contains a lot of 'technical debt'. Situations such as this create a divisive atmosphere, us against them, testers who feel that they are not listened to and developers who feel that testers are nit-picking about unimportant issues. Business stakeholders start resenting delivery teams for gold-plating the product when time is pressing, and delivery teams start resenting business stakeholders for insisting on an unsustainable pace of delivery. These disagreements are particularly problematic for delivery teams that are not in direct contact with customers.

It's easy to blame another group for being ignorant and causing this misunderstanding, but the real issue is that people often have a simplistic view of quality, and very rarely see the big picture. A good solution for this misunderstanding is to create a multi-layered, multi-faced view of quality that different groups can agree on.

One model that works relatively well in many situations is based on Maslow's hierarchy of human needs. The famous Maslow's hierarchy lists human needs as a pyramid with those necessary for basic functions (such as food, water) on the bottom level, safety (personal security, health, financial security), love and belonging (friendship, intimacy), and esteem (competence, respect) on the middle levels and self-actualisation (fulfilling one's potential) at the top. The premise of the hierarchy of needs is that when a lower-level need is not met, we disregard higher-level needs. For example, when a person doesn't have enough food, intimacy and respect, food is the most pressing thing. Another premise is that satisfying needs on the lower-levels of the pyramid brings diminishing returns after some point. Eating more food than we need brings obesity. More airport security than needed becomes a hassle. Our quality of life improves by satisfying higher-level needs after lower-level needs are satisfied. As with any other models, this one is an abstraction and it's easy to find all kinds of exceptions to it, but in general it captures the situation relatively well. We can do something similar for software.

Drawing parallels between the different levels of needs, we can create a pyramid of software quality levels:

1. Does it work at all? What are the key features, key technical qualities?
2. Does it work well? What are the key performance, security, scalability aspects?
3. Is it usable? What are the key usability scenarios?
4. Is it useful? What production metrics will show that it is used in real work?
5. Is it successful? What business metrics will show that this was worth doing? Is it operating within financial constraints?

Such a pyramid can help teams to define acceptance criteria at each of the levels, and create shared agreement on what the entire group means when they think about quality.

Key benefits

A shared visualisation of different aspects of quality helps to paint the big picture for everyone. People can avoid spending too much time improving aspects that are already de-risked to a satisfactory level. At the same time, everyone will understand what constitutes a critical problem – if any of the things in the pyramid is broken, it's pretty serious, regardless of what level it is on.

Although higher levels of the pyramid – typically characterised by production metrics, usage scenarios and operational constraints – might not be fully testable during development, they provide a useful context for designing the right solution and they might inform exploratory testing sessions.

How to make it work

The whole purpose of creating a shared big picture is to align expectations across different groups, so it only makes sense to do it in a cross-functional setting, with representatives of developers, testers, analysts and business stakeholders. Try to get senior representatives from each of those groups into a room, and draw the pyramid on a large whiteboard. Then let people add their expectations with sticky notes to each of the levels. After fifteen or twenty minutes, or when the discussion stops and people have no more ideas, go through the notes and try to quantify expectations. For example, if someone added 'people can quickly create documents' to the third level, define together what 'quickly' actually means.

We like doing such pyramids once per milestone, to guide work over the next three to six months. Items on the sticky notes should be relatively high level, representing global criteria and key activities, rather than low-level actions. Avoid trying to capture all possible test cases, and focus on the broad understanding that will allow you to make better low-level decisions later.

EXPLORE CAPABILITIES, NOT FEATURES

As software features are implemented, and user stories become ready for exploratory testing, it's only logical to base exploratory testing sessions on new stories or changed features. Although it might sound counter-intuitive, story-oriented exploratory testing sessions lead to tunnel vision and prevent teams from getting the most out of their effort.

Stories and features are a solid starting point for coming up with good deterministic checks. However, they aren't so good for exploratory testing. When exploratory testing is focused on a feature, or a set of changes delivered by a user story, people end up evaluating whether the feature works, and rarely stray off the path. In a sense, teams end up proving what they expect to see. However, exploratory testing is most powerful when it deals with the unexpected and the unknown. For this, we need to allow tangential observations and insights, and design new tests around unexpected discoveries. To achieve this, exploratory testing can't be focused purely on features.

Good exploratory testing deals with unexpected risks, and for this we need to look beyond the current piece of work. On the other hand, we can't cast the net too widely, because testing would lack focus. A good perspective for investigations that balances wider scope with focus is around user capabilities. Features provide capabilities to users to do something useful, or take away user capabilities to do something dangerous or damaging. A good way to look for unexpected risks is not to explore features, but related capabilities instead.

Key benefits

Focusing exploratory testing on capabilities instead of features leads to deeper insights and prevents tunnel vision. A good example is the contact form we built for MindMup. The related software feature was that a support request is sent when a user fills in the form. We could have explored the feature using multiple vectors, such as field content length, email formats, international character sets in the name or the message, but ultimately this would only focus on proving that the form worked. Casting the net a bit wider, we identified two capabilities related to the contact form:

- A user should be able to contact us for support easily in case of trouble. We should be able to support them easily, and solve their problems.
- Nobody should be able to block or break the contact channels for other users through intentional or unintentional misuse.

We set those capabilities as the focus of our exploratory testing session, and this led us to look at the accessibility of the contact form in case of trouble, and the ease of reporting typical problem scenarios. We discovered two critically important insights.

The first was that a major cause of trouble would not be covered by the initial solution. Flaky and unreliable network access was responsible for many incoming support requests. But when the Internet connection for users went down randomly, even though the form was filled in correctly, the browser might fail to connect to our servers. If someone suddenly went completely offline, the contact form wouldn't actually help at all. None of those situations should happen in an ideal world, but when they did, that's when users actually needed support. So the feature was implemented correctly, but there was still a big capability risk. This led us to offer an alternative contact channel for when the network was not accessible. We displayed the alternative contact email address prominently on the form, and also repeated it in the error message if the form submission failed.

The second big insight was that people might be able to contact us, but without knowing the internals of the application, they wouldn't be able to provide information for troubleshooting in case of data corruption or software bugs. That would pretty much leave us in the dark, and disrupt our ability to provide support. As a result, we decided not to even ask for common troubleshooting information, but instead obtain and send it automatically in the background. We also pulled out the last 1000 events that happened in the user interface, and sent them automatically with the support request, so that we could replay and investigate what exactly happened.

How to make it work

To get to good capabilities for exploring, brainstorm what a feature allows users to do, or what it prevents them from doing. When exploring user stories, try to focus on the user value part ('In order to...') rather than the feature description ('I want ...').

If you use impact maps for planning work, the third level of the map (actor impacts) are a good starting point for discussing capabilities. Impacts are typically changes to capabilities. If you use user story maps, the top-level item in the user story map spine related to the current user story is a nice starting point for discussion.

START WITH ALWAYS/NEVER

The first time a team works on a new component, or in an unfamiliar part of some business domain, they often face a chicken-and-egg situation in coming up with test ideas. Good examples can quickly lead to more good counter-examples, but people need at least a few good initial examples to get a broad picture of the entire problem space. When people work in an unfamiliar area, their lack of experience makes it's tricky to recognise when they have covered the basics and can start looking at more difficult boundaries. That is a dangerous situation because the whole team might think that they have identified all the key assumptions and ensured shared understanding, but their limited domain knowledge might prevent people from seeing horrible problems. In the famous Rumsfeld classification of knowledge, the 'unknown unknowns' could hide many problems and we might be blinded by our inexperience.

This is where the always/never heuristic is incredibly useful. In order to paint the big picture quickly, we often kick things off with a ten-minute session on identifying things that should always happen or that should never be allowed. This helps to set the stage for more interesting questions quickly, because absolute statements such as 'should always' and 'should never' urge people to come up with exceptions and edge cases.

For example, when working on the compliance part of an e-commerce system, we asked business stakeholders to write down a few things they felt should never happen. The first suggestion from a stakeholder was 'never lose a transaction'. This led to another statement, 'always audit a transaction', which then caused developers to ask if we should audit failed transactions as well. We then identified two opposing views of a transaction: business people regarded any attempt to buy anything as a transaction, even if the purchase was declined. But developers regarded only successful purchases as transactions. It turned out that it was actually quite important to capture attempted and failed purchases for fraud prevention purposes. Starting with always/never scenarios helped us quickly identify some wrong assumptions about the domain.

Key benefits

Absolute statements about a feature or a component are a great way to frame the discussion about key risks. Statements starting with 'always' or 'never' often point to the biggest business risks, and once people have analysed them, they have a much better context for understanding the rest of the functionality.

Another nice aspect of absolute statements is that they can easily be refuted – people have to find just one case when the statement is not true to invalidate it and open a good discussion. Because of this, writing down the absolute truths helps to surface different assumptions quickly, especially if someone easily comes up with counter-examples. This often points to differences in terminology or different mental models.

This is especially important for working on difficult legacy systems, because someone can quickly check whether the proposed truths are actually true for the old solution. For example, if a stakeholder claims that each purchase should lead to an audit record, we can quickly compare the number of purchases and the number of audit records for the previous six months in the legacy database. If they don't match, that is an interesting discovery about complex internal system interactions that people weren't aware of.

How to make it work

Because the discussion on absolute truths should lead to group discovery of different assumptions, try to avoid a single person being responsible for providing the list of all always/never statements. Split into several groups and brainstorm for ten or fifteen minutes separately, then bring groups together to compare results. Alternatively, give people sticky notes and let them write down ideas in silence for a while, then put all the notes on a wall and cluster together similar items.

Once you've identified the first batch of absolute truths, pick them up one by one and attempt to invalidate them. For each statement, try to come up with counter-examples or cases where the absolute truth might not hold. It's also interesting to list cases that could be easily misunderstood by someone with less domain experience, or without a good insight into internal workings. Those are good scenarios for feedback exercises and group discussions.

After discussing a statement about something that should never happen, remember to probe for alternative events (see the section Ask 'what happens instead?').

It goes without saying that any examples that violate a seemingly absolute truth should become critical test cases. But even if an absolute statement still holds true by the end of the discussion, capture the key scenarios that you've used to challenge it, and use them as tests in the future. Such examples protect against potential misunderstandings and wrong assumptions and are particularly useful to delivery team members with less domain experience.

As testers are usually very quick to point out, the happy path is just the tip of the iceberg when it comes to the types of tests needed for adequately covering the many risks of any new software feature.

Starting with the happy path scenario certainly makes sense, as it provides us with a strong initial key example and a basis from which to think about other possibilities, but we don't want to get stuck there.

It is not always easy to see what other paths to take, what other permutations to try and techniques to use. Commonly taught techniques like boundary value analysis and equivalence partitioning are good ways of flushing out specific tests and focusing coverage, but they are not enough in themselves.

Whether in a specification workshop, designing test ideas afterwards or in an exploratory test session, having a heuristic for test design can stimulate some very useful discussion and upturn some stones that otherwise might have been left untouched.

The heuristic we propose is based on nine emotions or types of behaviour: scary, happy, angry, delinquent, embarrassing, desolate, forgetful, indecisive, greedy, stressful. As a mnemonic, 'shaded figs' is the best we can come up with, but even if it is too long to remember what each one stands for, hopefully it will trigger the thought to look it up.

Key benefits

The 'shaded figs' heuristic helps teams design more complete tests, whether up-front, say in a specification workshop, or during an exploratory session. It stimulates new ideas for tests and exposes other areas of risk for consideration.

Using this spectrum of test type ideas can deliver good broad coverage pretty quickly when designing or executing tests. It can also be a nice reminder in a specification workshop if you are looking for alternatives to the initial key example and for negative cases from a variety of perspectives.

How to make it work

One way to make this work is to start with the happy path and look along it for alternatives. As we step through the happy path, start thinking of other paths that could be taken using on this checklist.

Have the heuristic by your side and refer to it or work through it as a team as you explore a story or feature.

Here is our set of emotional heuristics to stimulate test design, taking an emotional roller coaster of a ride along the way:

- *The scary path* – if this path was followed it would really tear the house down, and everything else with it. Flush out those areas of the highest risk to the stakeholders. Think what would scare each stakeholder the most about this piece of functionality or change.
- *The happy path* – the key example, positive test, that describes the straightforward case. This is the simplest path through the particular area of behaviour and functionality that we can think of, it is the simplest user interaction and we expect it to pass every time.
- *The angry path* – with the angry path we are looking for tests which we think will make the application react badly, throw errors and get cross with us for not playing nicely. These might be validation errors, bad inputs, logic errors.
- *The delinquent path* – consider the security risks that need testing, like authentication, authorisation, permissions, data confidentiality and so on.
- *The embarrassing path* – think of the things that, should they break, would cause huge embarrassment all round. Even if they wouldn't be an immediate catastrophe in loss of business,

they might have a significant impact on credibility, internally or externally. This could be as simple as something like spelling quality as 'Qality', as we once saw on a testing journal (just think of the glee on all those testers' faces).

- *The desolate path* – provide the application or component with bleakness. Try zeros, nulls, blanks or missing data, truncated data and any other kind of incomplete input, file or event that might cause some sort of equally desolate reaction.
- *The forgetful path* – fill up all the memory and CPU capacity so that the application has nowhere left to store anything. See how forgetful it becomes and whether it starts losing data.
- *The indecisive path* – simulate being an indecisive user, unable to quite settle on one course of action. Turn things on and off, clicking back buttons on the browser, move between breadcrumb trails with half-entered data. These kinds of actions can cause errors in what the system remembers as the last known state.
- *The greedy path* – select everything, tick every box, opt into every option, order lots of everything, just generally load up the functionality with as much of everything as it allows to see how it behaves.
- *The stressful path* – find the breaking point of the functions and components so you can see what scale of solution you currently have and give you projections for future changes in business volumes.

This technique works really well in specification workshops when multiple people are present, because the non-happy-path ideas are likely to generate interesting conversations, asking questions that have not been thought of yet and that are hard to answer. Some questions may need to be taken away and investigated further (non-functional characteristics repeatedly have this tendency).

TEST BENEFIT AS WELL AS IMPLEMENTATION

User stories often impact several features, and a single feature can be extended and modified by many user stories. Because of this, acceptance criteria for a story are often organised around individual features, and expressed in terms of technical impacts. This design makes a lot of sense for long-term maintenance (see the section *Avoid organising tests by work items*), but it also introduces the risk of losing the big picture.

For example, imagine a story about upgrading the video codec library for a teleconferencing system. The story might imply a range of integration tests to ensure that commands are sent correctly. It would probably imply a large number of regression checks to ensure that the new library supports all the critical features of the old library. Taken together, these two groups of tests prove that we upgraded the library correctly, but this does not necessarily mean that the story is done. One of our colleagues worked on such a story,

prompted by user complaints about video quality. The completed story was delivered to production, the team declared victory and moved on, but the complaints kept coming in. The problem was that the proposed solution (library upgrade) looked good as a prototype, but did not really solve the video quality problems. Because of the technical complexity of the story, the team got lost in the details and never measured whether the overall solution was complete.

This issue is particularly problematic for larger teams, or organisations where a single story is delivered by multiple teams.

Usually even when there are overall tests that show how individual parts of a story come together, they are still described in terms of the implementation. For example, a user story that introduces a new report might be broken down into lots of small data filter tasks or column calculation rules, and there would be one overall test executing the entire report. But another test is needed, one that checks that the benefits are actually delivered to the users.

To expand on this example, if the initial assumption was that a different report would help users to identify trade exceptions faster, the final test could create a few historically recorded exceptions and check how quickly they can be identified using the report.

Key benefits

When teams describe an overall test through a potential benefit, rather than using implementation details, they can spot missing functionality and bad solutions. In a sense, individual tests allow us to check if we did what we agreed to do, but the overall benefit test checks if the thing we agreed to do was actually a good solution.

For example, while working on MindMup, we had a story about enabling conference speakers to create storyboards from mind maps. The expected benefit was that speakers could use a mind map to prepare the first version of their conference talk slides. Because it was a pretty big story, we sliced it down into several smaller stories, then broke those stories down into twenty or so tasks, and attached tests to the tasks. When all the tests passed, theoretically the story was done. However, we also had two overall tests. One of them specified that it should now be possible to assemble a set of slides for a typical conference presentation. Using my typical talks as a guideline, this meant 25 to 30 slides, most of them containing an image. Running this test at the end, we discovered that the server-side components fell over due to memory consumption. We had to go

back to the drawing board and implement several new features, such as image caching and different work distribution between server and client components, to really complete the story.

How to make it work

Instead of just asking 'does it work?' when discussing overall story tests, ask 'how would you know if it actually works well?' Try to define what 'good enough' means in terms of capabilities and benefits, without tying it to a particular technical solution or implementation. In the video teleconferencing example, the overall benefit test could have been expressed as an improved bit-rate or a reduction in dropped video frames for a particular customer segment.

In *Fifty Quick Ideas To Improve your User Stories*, we propose that stories should try to describe a behaviour change. If your stories describe behaviour changes, then design tests around those changes. Measure the capability or potential to achieve such a change before deployment, for example, can a knowledgeable user now discover trade exceptions faster? Consider checking whether the benefit was actually delivered to real users after the story was shipped to production. Checking the benefits in actual use is the final test that can confirm whether the solution was actually any good.

Overall benefits tests do not necessarily need to be managed the same way as the other story tests. Even if the expected benefit is completely deterministic, you might get more value out of running manual exploratory tests around it instead of automating the checks. Testing if something works well often leads to tangential information discovery, and unattended automated execution won't provide that learning.

Qualities that are difficult to measure, such as usability or performance, rarely get the testing attention they deserve. They are mostly inspected as an afterthought, typically when someone complains. Even then, because there is no clear success criteria, it's difficult to prove that problems have been completely fixed.

Teams often don't even bother capturing or specifying stakeholders' expectations for aspects that are difficult to test, apart from vague statements such as 'It has to be fast'. Without a clear set of expectations, any discussions on features or improvements become highly subjective, and different people have different ideas about how well the system needs to perform. This leads to unchecked wrong assumptions, design problems, subjective arguments between stakeholders and delivery team members and generally a lot of misunderstanding.

Just because something is difficult to test, we shouldn't give up on capturing or expressing expectations. If an aspect of a system is difficult to test, this should not prevent people from discussing how well the system needs to perform before development starts. Even if you're not going to actively measure an important aspect of quality, try to quantify it.

Key benefits

Quantifying key aspects of quality helps teams have better design discussions. A requirement for the homepage of a website to load in under two seconds with 50,000 concurrent users needs a completely different technical solution than a requirement to load in under ten seconds when 5,000 people are online. Without a clear quantified target, it's impossible to choose between the two options, so teams might end up either delivering an underperforming system, or wasting time unnecessarily gold-plating it.

Even if something can't be measured easily or cheaply before delivery, it can often be evaluated cheaply after it is shipped. This can help inform future product management decisions. For example, if a team wanted to improve average homepage load time, they could monitor actual system performance in production, compare it to expectations, then come up with a target improvement. If the target improvement is quantified, product managers can decide easily if it has been delivered, or if they need to prioritise more performance improvement work. This helps to avoid over-investing in aspects that are already good enough.

Finally, when an aspect of quality is quantified, teams can better evaluate the cost and difficulty of measuring. For example, we quantified a key usability scenario for MindMup as 'Novice users will be able to create and share simple mind maps in under five minutes'. Once the definition was that clear, it turned out not to be so impossible or expensive to measure it. We often approach random people at conferences and ask them to try out new versions of the system, and measure how long it takes them to create and share a simple map.

How to make it work

A good way to start quantifying difficult aspects is to try to capture key representative scenarios that are good indicators of speed. Work with stakeholders to identify them. For example, instead of just saying that a website needs to be fast, select scenarios such as initial access to the homepage, browsing and searching for products, and checking out with a shopping cart.

It's likely that all such scenarios have slightly different target performance requirements. A homepage might need to load in less than two seconds, but shopping cart checkout might be fine taking ten seconds. Once the key scenarios are listed, identify the conditions that might impact the scenarios. For example, the number of concurrent users has a huge impact on the cost of speeding up a web page. Lastly, work with stakeholders to capture their expectations under various example conditions. For example, investigate expected homepage load times when 5,000 users are looking at it, or when 50,000 suddenly decide to hit your site. It's also useful to specify a percentage of success, such as '99% of the time', or '99.999% of the time'. This also helps to establish good service level agreements for monitoring production systems.

Another useful trick is to try defining such expectations as intervals instead of discrete values. For example, instead of saying that the homepage needs to load in under four seconds, specify that it should be at least under four seconds but does not need to be under two. This provides clarity for design discussions, so that the team can come up with solutions that will scale nicely.

Once you know the key scenarios, it's often useful to gather competitor or market data about them, as a way of depersonalising the discussions. It's much easier to argue a case for a specific target if some aspect needs to exceed or match the market leaders than it is if you are trying to nail a target out of the blue sky. A particularly good way to start such discussions is to use the QUPER model, which visually compares proposed solutions to market utility, differentiation and saturation levels. For more information on this, see our book *Fifty Quick Ideas To Improve Your User Stories* and *quper.org*.

ORGANISE TEST IDEAS USING AN ACC MATRIX

In order to deliver frequently, teams need to have a clear idea of when it is safe to release a new version of software. However, with frequent deliveries, the time available for testing is scarce, and it's difficult to establish a clear, impartial and objective criterion for how much testing is enough. It's easy to say that all automated tests need to pass, but teams rarely have a clear idea about how much additional exploratory testing is required. To add insult to injury, frequent delivery pretty much guarantees that the system is changing faster than it's possible to keep test documentation up to date.

Story maps and impact maps lose value after the related software milestone is delivered, but the list of changes implemented as part of the milestone needs to be preserved for future regression testing. Without a good way to capture that information, teams keep previous backlog plans lying around, and try to manage exploratory testing using past work items. This causes the same problems for exploratory testing as for automated tests, as described in *Avoid organising tests by work items*. In order to be able to prioritise and coordinate testing, we need an effective way to capture and organise information about what the system does now which can easily incorporate future changes.

This is where the attribute-component-capability matrix comes into play. The attribute-component-capability (ACC) matrix is a technique for visualising and organising test ideas and risk information, developed by James Whittaker during his work at Microsoft and Google, and described in *How Google Tests Software*. The ACC matrix charts different capabilities in relation to system components and

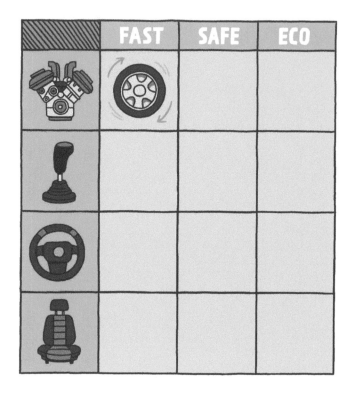

quality attributes. It is a table in which columns have the names of quality attributes, system components are represented by rows, and system capabilities provided by the components to satisfy quality attributes sit in the table cells. For example, in the ACC matrix for MindMup we capture the fact that the Amazon S3 integration (component) allows users to save simple mind maps without registering (capability) to make the experience frictionless (attribute). The capability is captured in a cell at the intersection of the 'Frictionless' column and the 'Amazon S3' row. A single cell can contain multiple related capabilities.

Key benefits

ACC is a quick and iterative way to establish a test plan that is easily maintainable in the future. The list of system components and the set of quality attributes tend to change much less frequently than the related features, so an ACC matrix provides a relatively stable structure for discussions and prioritisation. As user stories are delivered, the related capabilities can easily be added to the matrix if needed.

The links between components and capabilities help teams to see where to concentrate their testing effort when a part of the system changes. For example, for MindMup we have a policy of exploring all medium-risk capabilities linked to any component that changes, and all critical capabilities linked to other components.

Because quality attributes and capabilities are easier to compare and evaluate than features, each capability in an ACC matrix can have a risk score agreed by multiple stakeholders. This helps teams effectively capture the risk profile of a large system and inform testing activities. Ideally, the ACC matrix should describe at a high level everything people could test with an infinite amount of time and money available. Teams can then use the matrix to create an objective, impartial criterion for what makes a system releasable under a particular testing budget. Even better, rather than establishing only one criterion, an ACC matrix also allows people to quickly plan different testing activities around different development cycles, by using diferent paths through the matrix. Teams can decide what the criteria are for major upgrades and smaller releases, and what should be done periodically to test less risky items.

How to make it work

The biggest challenge in creating an ACC matrix is identifying and capturing capabilities. While system attributes and components tend to be easy to identify, capabilities are more difficult. They should be relatively high-level, and they might describe a whole range of scenarios. For example, the capability of saving simple mind maps includes saving new maps, updating old maps, saving maps with right-to-left text, saving maps with images and regional character sets and so on. The key aspect of good capabilities is that they are testable, but a single capability shouldn't fully describe a test case. Avoid putting in specific data or values in capabilities.

In *How Google Tests Software*, the authors suggest the following guidelines for identifying capabilities:

- Write a capability as an action, ideally from the sense of a user accomplishing some task
- Provide enough information for a tester to understand what variables are involved in the related test cases, and do not aim to provide full details of the test cases.
- A capability should work together with other capabilities. Don't aim to describe a use case or a user story with a single capability.

If you're using user story maps to organise the backlog of work, the activities listed in the backbone of the story maps are a good starting point for identifying capabilities. If you're using an impact map, then investigate the behaviours changed or enhanced by the items on the third level (impacts) of the map.

USE RISK CHECKLISTS FOR CROSS-CUTTING CONCERNS

Tests for wide cross-cutting concerns are often tricky to describe, because they generally apply across a broad set of features. For example, look and feel should ideally be consistent across all input screens in an application. Describing look and feel individually for each form is an overkill, and introduces unnecessary duplication. That's why teams often put aspects such as usability and performance outside the normal testing activities and handle them separately.

However, just testing such things at a global level causes teams to miss the peculiarities of how they relate to a particular feature, and delay feedback. Small updates to features might not pose a big risk to cross-cutting concerns, so running a whole set of cross-cutting tests might not be needed every time. But some changes might actually introduce a lot of risk and have a huge impact. Without some kind of test plan, it's almost impossible to evaluate the impact on a case-by-case basis and prioritise tests. Leaving global concerns

to a separate testing cycle prevents teams from doing effective short iterative cycles that identify impacts. With cross-cutting concerns, the same risks and test ideas apply to a large set of things to test, leading to a lot of repetition and routine work, regardless of whether the tests are automated or manual. In the *Checklist Manifesto*, Atul Gawande talks about the risks of routine and repetitive tasks in a complex environment, where experts are up against two main difficulties. The first is that human memory and attention are not that great. That's why people tend to overlook mundane and routine tasks when there is something else that seems more important. The second is that people talk themselves into skipping steps under time pressure, even when they remember them.

Trying to capture all cross-cutting concerns with deterministic checks is overkill and leads to too many repetitive tests, causing test maintenance problems. Leaving those risks for manual testing requires good guidelines on what to test, and a solid plan that can be evaluated and reviewed on a case-by-case basis. This is where effective checklists play a crucial role.

The big trick to make such checklists work is to avoid listing individual test scenarios. Checklists with detailed scenarios or steps grow too long to be practical over time. They cause people to turn their brains off and follow a set of instructions, instead of using their expertise and intuition to prioritise and select risks to explore. The most useful global checklists spell out the key risks, and serve as a reminder for experts.

Instead of describing individual test scenarios, try to name the key risks in global checklists.

Key benefits

Global risk checklists remind and inspire people to explore the right things, and prevent them from skipping critical risks, while allowing for individual variation. They allow teams to effectively prioritise and plan tests within short iterative cycles. Teams can consider checklists in the context of individual impacts, and decide which risks need to be covered to address overall concerns after a small feature change. Because the checklists do not specify test steps, teams can decide on the best way to address each risk. This leads to better focused tests, and does not require expensive test maintenance for individual scenarios.

Having a clear list of risks for each cross-cutting concern allows teams to speed up their user story discussions. Instead of coming up with the same things over and over, people can quickly go through a checklist and discuss how the items on it apply to a particular feature. They can also consider the risks in the context of a particular change and evaluate whether there are any specific impacts to test for.

An additional benefit of reviewing checklists before each user story is that people are more likely to note problems and offer solutions. Gawande quotes research from the Johns Hopkins hospital in Baltimore, where they noticed this effect with using checklists for surgery procedures. This effect is known as an 'activation phenomenon', where giving people a chance to say something at the start activates their sense of participation and responsibility, and their willingness to speak up.

How to make it work

Gawande says that good checklists should not aim to be comprehensive how-to guides, but need to be 'quick and simple tools to buttress the skills of expert professionals'. He advises creating checklists that are five to nine items long, because that is the limit of people's working memory. This means that it's better to have several sets of small, focused checklists, instead of one huge list. We tend to create one checklist for each critical concern, and if one of the lists becomes too big, split it into a set of more focused lists. For example, an overall usability checklist for a website would probably be too long, but a usability checklist for input forms rarely needs to be more than ten items long.

Avoid checklists that are used to tick items off as people work (Gawande calls those Read-Do lists). Instead, aim to create lists that allow people to work, then pause and review to see if they missed anything ('Do-Confirm' in Gawande's terminology).

DOCUMENT TRUST BOUNDARIES

Complex systems often suffer from trust issues. When teams work on small pieces of a larger system, it's rarely easy to know how much they can trust components created by other teams. If a team trusts too much, they open themselves up to code from the other teams introducing weird issues that are difficult to troubleshoot. If a team trusts too little, they can waste time on building defences against threats that don't exist, and testing features that are already being verified somewhere else.

For example, a payroll processing system needs a list of employees and their contractual salaries to calculate net payments. In a large system, the employee data typically comes from a component maintained by a completely different team. If we suspect that this component might give us duplicate records, people without an account number, or invalid salary amounts, the payroll component needs to be able to identify

problematic records, issue alerts on them, and provide some way of resolving inconsistencies. All these features need to be properly tested as well. However, if we know that the other team has things under control, and that the employee data is solid, then we don't need to discuss and specify how to handle data problems. Checking for such conditions would be a waste of time and resources. To add insult to injury, it's often the cross-component integration tests that are the bulkiest, the most fragile, the slowest and the most expensive to maintain.

Trust boundaries change over time – something that was unreliable can be cleaned up, and something that we trusted implicitly can be messed up. When dependencies are managed by different teams, changes in internals that might cause problems are rarely communicated. For example, the employee data component might start supporting external import, and suddenly low-quality data might start entering the system. The team that manages the payroll component won't know about the change until weird problems appear with payments and someone reports a bug.

Trust problems can happen within a single team, not just across different teams. Developers usually know system internals better than business stakeholders, and testers are typically more aware of past problems than developers. These knowledge gaps often lead to different assumptions about potential problems and the scope of development and testing. The groups can have different implied trust boundaries, leading to much disagreement between business stakeholders, testers and developers. Less trusting people are blamed for inventing impossible edge cases and nitpicking, while more trusting team members are blamed for being ignorant and not caring about quality.

To prevent such trust issues, explicitly identify and document trust boundaries as a group, including developers, testers and business stakeholders. Once the trust boundaries are agreed, it becomes easy to decide whether a particular module needs strong defences and we need to make decisions about all sorts of weird data cases, or if we can just focus on the common scenarios and get on with the work.

Key benefits

Identifying and documenting trust boundaries allows teams to set up a common discussion framework for expected behaviour. This helps to avoid unproductive disagreements on whether people are nitpicking or ignoring a potential disaster. It helps people differentiate between a normal invalid input and a genuine unexpected exception. Not only do we avoid duplicate tests and speed up feedback where we can

trust more, we can also design and build more resilient systems where we have to trust less.

Explicitly stated boundaries allow teams to react more effectively to unexpected violations, because it is easy to identify related tests that need to be revisited.

How to make it work

Before starting a discussion on a feature or a system area, discuss and note down how much you trust other teams or third parties to set the context. Then design checks and specifications within the specified trust boundary. Plan exploratory tests to probe the boundary and try to break it, to see if it really holds.

In *Explore It*, Elisabeth Hendrickson advises running a 'what if?' question session to probe boundaries.

It's useful to put a note about the trust boundary on integration tests for future reference. When you amend a test, investigate whether the documented boundaries still hold.

In larger organisations, it's also a good idea to set up triggers and alerts for trust boundary violations, so you can at least react appropriately when a different team does something unexpected. Some examples that work well are validating consistency at system boundaries and sending email notifications to developers, or raising alerts when unexpected data crops up in the production environment.

Finally, watch out for bugs that point to violations of trust boundaries. Instead of just fixing one such bug and moving on, revisit all related tests around the same boundary and see if any other features need to be discussed.

MONITOR TRENDS IN LOGS AND CONSOLES

28

The internal workings of complex systems are not easy to control and analyse, especially if the developers working on one part have no influence over other parts. This is why it will never be possible to specify a complete set of tests for a complex system. We never know what else is there, and what unexpected variables might cause problems. Small changes don't necessarily manifest immediately, but compound effects can be huge. And such compound effects are particularly tricky to analyse, because combined symptoms are often misleading, and one person seldom has the entire picture. And, of course, compound problems tend to show up at the worst possible moment.

A year or so ago, Gojko had a relatively long stop-over between two flights in Paris, planning to use it to grab some decent food in the city. But the Internet pixies had other plans. As soon as Gojko turned on his phone after landing, a ton of email alerts and customer complaints came through. Instead of a hot lunch at a nice quiet restaurant, he ended up hot-fixing a production system in a noisy, crowded airport. Weird, complex problems somehow always show up at the worst possible moment. MindMup integration with Google Drive Realtime API had mysteriously stopped working, without any changes on our side, and an unstable airport wifi made troubleshooting particularly difficult. At the end, it turned out that two event notifications were now being fired differently, and the system interpreted the new sequence wrongly as lack of privileges to access files.

Although it's easy to blame a third party for changing their API without telling anyone, in retrospect there was no need for this to cause a huge outage. In fact, we had had plenty of warnings but we had just ignored them. We monitor end-user errors and warnings to check for unexpected problems, and there had been occasional spikes of privilege errors with the Realtime API over the previous month, but we had just dismissed them as people trying to access files without being logged in. The fact that they were spikes probably meant it was the API developers gradually releasing the new version of their software and fixing it. If we had known what to look for, the problem was perfectly preventable.

Many systems have logs, monitoring consoles or automated end-user error reports, but these are mostly used for troubleshooting and diagnostics when users report problems. To prevent really tricky compound problems from accumulating, review such system outputs periodically, or monitor them using automated tools to look for unexpected trends. Look for errors, exception stack traces or warnings in system logs and consoles during testing. You might spot early signs of trouble before anyone else. After the airport hot-fixing episode, we created a monitoring system for error spikes. Six months later, it warned us about strange Dropbox integration errors. We caught a change in their API and fixed it before any of our users started complaining.

Key benefits

Apart from including early warnings about potential compound problems, system logs and consoles are often the only reliable source of information about what really goes on in complex workflows or systems with many components. Tracing through a log can provide useful insights on what else needs to be checked or explored after a software change. A client of ours was extending a financial trading platform built by a third party, and they were never sure which platform services were involved in the workflows that had to be modified. We would run a trade through the system, and then inspect system logs to see which services printed log notifications. This helped us catch unforeseen impacts many times. Logs and consoles can provide fantastic insights about what additional tests you need to write.

How to make it work

Many infrastructural components and tools today come with ready-made consoles. For example, all popular browsers have a JavaScript console (sometimes called error console), and most server software has some kind of troubleshooting console you can connect to using TCP. Servers also often support a way to remotely capture logs. Whenever possible, have a system console or log monitor open during exploratory testing, and try to read through the outputs caused by your actions. There will probably be a lot of garbage there, but you will at least learn what to expect and be able to spot new trends or events out of the normal.

For automated tests, it's more useful to keep an eye on file sizes. For example, if a test suite run normally generates 20 KB of logs, and the most recent execution dumped 200 KB, something important changed. Maybe the change is perfectly OK, but it deserves investigating.

Any but the most trivial systems built today involve multiple components and networking, so they are designed to be fault tolerant and some errors are normal. For example, a web system might log database access errors and reconnect automatically. Production logs have some normal error log trends, so early warnings about unexpected complex faults can be difficult to spot. A good trick to make them stand out is to log all exceptions, errors and warnings and break them down into groups for monitoring. That way it's easy to spot unusual trends. For example, the monitoring console for MindMup shows errors grouped by external API used, and we show the number of errors, number of timeouts and number of total requests each day. Due to networking, browser issues and a ton of other factors outside of our control, some small percentage of requests will fail or time out each day. But if one of those figures starts growing differently from the others, we know there is a problem to investigate.

MOB YOUR TEST SESSIONS

When planning or designing tests, a single person can think of many scenarios. However, any individual quickly finds diminishing returns in generating valuable new ideas for tests. We tend to lean towards the same techniques and types of tests (we can't help thinking the way we think), covering one class of risks well, but not others. It becomes an exercise in creating remote edge cases that have little practical value in terms of risk mitigation.

The same can be true for running testing sessions. A single person's gaze is naturally drawn to the specific thing under test, making it hard to see other simultaneous behaviours in the product. A pair provides wider visibility, but the partner is likely to be drawn into focusing on the same goal. Also, in many paired sessions, the person who isn't actively testing is scribing notes and observing what the active person is doing. This consumes time and brain power.

Instead of working alone, try running a mobbed testing session. Involve a group of people, maybe your whole team or a wider group including members from other teams or other stakeholders.

Use mobbed test design to generate lots of test ideas rapidly, which can be easily distilled down to the most valuable tests for automating. Or use it in exploratory sessions for fast group feedback and spotting directional changes needed, assessment of multiple areas and getting powerful consensus on risks and quality.

Key benefits

This approach generates lots of ideas for tests very quickly, much more quickly than an individual or pair can. This diversity of thought results in a far greater range of coverage. Mobbed test design provides the fastest possible feedback and identification of directional changes needed so that you are always addressing the biggest risks and extracting the most valuable information.

With a mob, you have the ability to diverge into multiple strands when more than one avenue of exploration opens up and then merge again, all within the same session. An interesting effect we've found involving people outside the immediate team is that their lack of prior knowledge allows for some freer and more radical test design, uncovering information and defects that would never have been found by the smaller team.

Mobbed testing sessions are also a good way of opening up more cross-team and departmental collaboration, improving relationships and increasing the exchange of approaches and ideas.

How to make it work

Start with the scope and purpose of the session. Is it for a specific feature, user story, defect or area of weakness in the system, or is it product wide? Decide on an appropriate level of preparation for the session: details about the requirement, acceptance criteria, the design, the test environment and data concerns, the information objectives, and so on.

Decide who to invite: the whole team, customer representatives, another team, sales or marketing (remember diversity breeds fresh ideas). Think about the number of people, how to arrange the area to engage everyone, how to structure and facilitate the session. The majority of mobbed sessions we've attended have involved between four and eight people. They can still work well with as many as 20 to 30 people, though

for a larger number think about diverging into smaller groups and merging again to ensure information is collected and shared. Smaller sessions allow for more informality and a more natural sharing of feedback. In any case set clear information objectives and a time-box to give some bounds and direction.

Start by explaining the requirement, product, feature, problem statement, design and any other useful context to get everyone involved up to speed.

For a test design session just start coming up with test ideas, don't try to remove duplicates or theme them too early, leave this to the end so as not constrain people. Keep people thinking of ideas for slightly longer than seems comfortable. After quickly generating the most obvious ideas, people will start to dry up. If you let them think for a bit longer, rather than stopping straight away, some unusual but potentially very valuable ideas will almost certainly emerge, exposing new risks, requirement gaps or design limitations. Collect all the ideas generated then group, refine and risk-prioritise them (likelihood and impact).

Experiment with the format of your mobbed testing sessions. Many start by someone giving a tour of the feature, working through some typical routes while the supporting cast observe, take notes, request information and flag areas for investigation. It becomes more interesting when the mob requests closer inspection of something. For example someone tries to run a report that demonstrates a newly designed test, and the report doesn't contain the expected information. The group calls out additional test ideas to try out. Some may split off to investigate possible causes in the code or the group might split in two to follow up on different lines of enquiry.

The larger group size allows exploration of different ideas and testing many theories within the bounds of a single session, whilst keeping constant communication with each other and merging periodically to align to the session objectives.

Consider having a whiteboard to scribe notes and ideas down on. A single notepad does not allow communication of ideas as easily for a large group.

DON'T LET THE PEN
BE THE BOTTLENECK

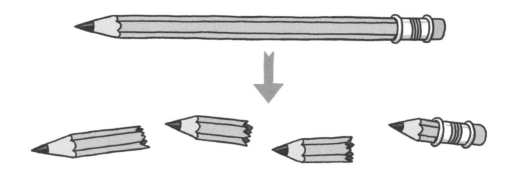

Sometimes specification workshops are less like collaborative brainstorming and more like lectures, with one 'expert' doing all the talking and writing, and others standing around watching. This can be quite off-putting and prevent people from engaging.

This also happens by accident when the person leading the walkthrough of stories has over-prepared for the session, for example, they might have already designed the key examples and then present them to the team at the group session. When they want these examples to be scrutinised and challenged, they actually find that the other attendees don't offer constructive criticism because it appears that the specification has already been finished.

Whatever the reason, when there is a single pen being wielded by one person, it can be very difficult for a group to get into the flow of collaboration, idea generation and constructive criticism.

If this happens at your specification workshops, give everyone a pen so that they can write on the whiteboard or flipchart, and encourage them all to stand within writing range of the board. As soon as someone has an idea, they can get it out in the open for everyone to see, understand, build upon or improve.

Key benefits

This idea is especially useful for overcoming 'alpha dog' behaviour, where one person tends to dominate the discussions, limiting the opportunity for other members to contribute or challenge ideas. Simply giving everyone a pen can level the playing field and make everyone feel equally entitled to contribute their views and ideas.

By giving everyone the mechanism to write their ideas down quickly, the differences between assumptions from different people become more visible. Changes and crossed-out values are evidence that our first thoughts were not correct, or that there was disagreement or a lack of shared understanding in the group. These are exactly the areas and examples that merit deeper examination or discussion, as these conflicts and disagreements are pointers to areas of risk in our feature, and need to be resolved.

This also helps the collaboration process to become much quicker and more productive. One person's idea or example immediately sparks thoughts in other people's minds, and they can enhance the idea or fine-tune the details quickly themselves, without having to give instructions to the person with the pen.

How to make it work

When you hold a specification workshop, always start with a low-tech medium, such as whiteboards or flipcharts, and transfer your cleaned-up results to a tool later. Our thinking about a problem is influenced by the medium we use to capture our ideas and examples. When people use a word processor, they tend to be verbose and use fewer concrete examples, because tables can be a hassle to create. When using Excel, teams have the opposite problem. They try to make relationships formulaic and avoid descriptions, because composing and formatting text nicely is a hassle.

For workshops involving larger groups, split the team into at least two groups. We find that limiting each group to three or four people, ideally with a mix of roles in each, gives the best results. Each group can work on the same problem independently, then reconvene to compare progress and ideas.

Give each person a different coloured pen (but avoid light colours that are harder to see). If you are using regular whiteboards, keep a stock of working whiteboard pens, as fading pens are a great source of frustration when people are trying to get the discussion going. Fine-point Sharpies are good for flipcharts or portable whiteboard sheets, and are sometimes a better alternative than whiteboard pens, as using them keeps the signs of battle visible. If you are using whiteboard pens, encourage people to cross values out initially rather than erasing them, for this reason.

Make sure each person has enough room to see and access the whiteboard or flipchart easily. This is another reason why small groups work best. Even when everyone is standing up, if there are five or more people, someone can end up being on the periphery and perhaps less engaged in the discussion.

Encourage multi-tasking to find a lot of examples quickly: discuss the first few cases together, but as you get into the flow, let people add new examples simultaneously. Once everyone's ideas have been captured, pause the group and check for duplication and conflicts to identify key examples.

Try silent reviews: when your sheet is full of examples, silently review your work and consider what needs correcting or improving, or which examples are not as informative as the others, and mark these with your pen. Discuss them when everyone has had time to think for themselves.

Finally, remember that even the shape of the blank space in front of us influences the way we fill that space. For example, when we conduct training, and give different groups the same problem to discuss, those groups given a landscape-oriented flipchart sheet tend to create examples using a sequence style ('A then B then C'), those given a portrait-oriented sheet tend to create tables with only a few columns, and those given a large whiteboard often create a comprehensive matrix of possibilities, simply because the space encourages it. Change the orientation of your flipchart paper and see if that leads to subtle changes in the way you express your examples.

SNOOP ON THE COMPETITION

As a general rule, teams focus the majority of testing activities on their zone of control, on the modules they develop, or the software that they are directly delivering. But it's just as irresponsible not to consider competition when planning testing as it is in the management of product development in general, whether the field is software or consumer electronics.

Software products that are unique are very rare, and it's likely that someone else is working on something similar to the product or project that you are involved with at the moment. Although the products might be built using different technical platforms and address different segments, key usage scenarios probably translate well across teams and products, as do the key risks and major things that can go wrong.

When planning your testing activities, look at the competition for inspiration – the cheapest mistakes to fix are the ones already made by other people. Although it might seem logical that people won't openly disclose information about their mistakes, it's actually quite easy to get this data if you know where to look.

Teams working in regulated industries typically have to submit detailed reports on problems caught by users in the field. Such reports are kept by the regulators and can typically be accessed in their archives. Past regulatory reports are a priceless treasure trove of information on what typically goes wrong, especially because of the huge financial and reputation impact of incidents that are escalated to such a level.

For teams that do not work in regulated environments, similar sources of data could be news websites or even social media networks. Users today are quite vocal when they encounter problems, and a quick search for competing products on Facebook or Twitter might uncover quite a few interesting testing ideas. Complaints in online reviews are also very informative.

Lastly, most companies today operate free online support forums for their customers. If your competitors have a publicly available bug tracking system or a discussion forum for customers, sign up and monitor it. Look for categories of problems that people typically inquire about and try to translate them to your product, to get more testing ideas.

For high-profile incidents that have happened to your competitors, especially ones in regulated industries, it's often useful to conduct a fake post-mortem. Imagine that a similar problem was caught by users of your product in the field and reported to the news. Try to come up with a plausible excuse for how it might have happened, and hold a fake retrospective about what went wrong and why such a problem would be allowed to escape undetected. This can help to significantly tighten up testing activities.

Key benefits

Investigating competing services and products and their problems is a cheap way of getting additional testing ideas, not about theoretical risks that might happen, but about things that actually happened to someone else in the same market segment. This is incredibly useful for teams working on a new piece of software or an unfamiliar part of the business domain, when they can't rely on their own historical data or knowledge for inspiration.

Running a fake post-mortem can help to discover blind spots and potential process improvements, both in software testing and in support activities. High-profile problems often surface because information falls through the cracks in an organisation, or people do not have sufficiently powerful tools to inspect and observe the software in use. Thinking about a problem that happened to someone else and translating it to your situation can help establish checks and make the system more supportable, so that problems do not escalate to that level. Such activities also communicate potential risks to a larger group of people, so developers can be more aware of similar risks when they design the system, and testers can get additional testing ideas to check.

The post-mortem suggestions, especially around improving the support procedures or observability, help the organisation to handle 'black swans' – unexpected and unknown incidents that won't be prevented by any kind of regression testing. We can't know upfront what those risks are (or they wouldn't be unexpected), but we can train the organisation to react faster and better to such incidents. This is akin to government disaster relief organisations holding simulations of floods and earthquakes to discover facilitation and coordination problems. It's much cheaper and less risky to discover things like this in a safe simulated environment than learn about organisational cracks when the disaster actually happens.

How to make it work

When investigating support forums, look for patterns and categories rather than individual problems. Due to different implementations and technology choices, it's unlikely that third-party product issues will directly translate to your situation, but problem trends or areas of influence will probably be similar.

One particularly useful trick is to look at the root cause analyses in the reports, and try to identify similar categories of problems in your software that could be caused by the same root causes.

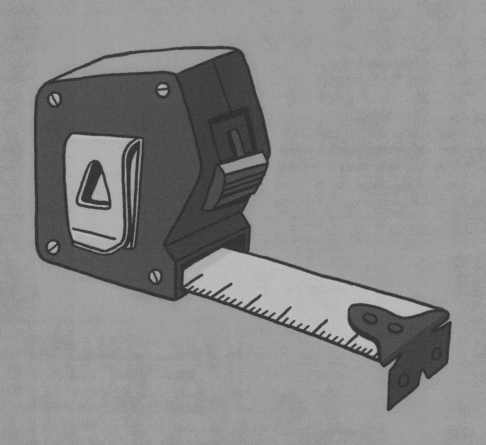

FIFTY
Quick
IDEAS

DESIGNING GOOD CHECKS

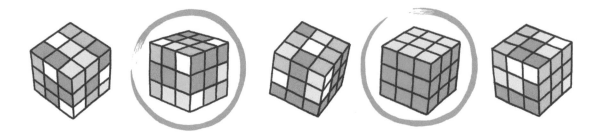

User stories need clear, precise and testable acceptance criteria so that they can be objectively measured. At the same time, regardless of how many scenarios teams use for testing, there are always more things that can be tested. It can be tempting to describe acceptance criteria with loads of scenarios, and look at all possible variations for the sake of completeness. Although trying to identify all possible variations might seem to lead to more complete testing and better stories, this is a sure way to destroy a good user story.

Because fast iterative work does not allow time for unnecessary documentation, acceptance criteria often doubles as a specification. If this specification is complex and difficult to understand, it is unlikely to lead to good results. Complex specifications don't invite discussion. People tend to read such documents alone and selectively ignore parts which they feel are less important. This does not really create shared understanding, but instead just provides an illusion of precision and completeness.

A typical example is on the right. This one was followed by ten more pages of similar stuff.

```
Feature: Payment routing

Scenario: Visa Electron, Austria
  Given the card is 4568 7197 3938 2020
  When the payment is made
  The selected gateway is Enterpayments-V2

Scenario: Visa Electron, Germany
  Given the card is 4468 7197 3939 2928
  When the payment is made
  The selected gateway is Enterpayments-V1

Scenario: Visa Electron, UK
  Given the card is 4218 9303 0309 3990
  When the payment is made
  The selected gateway is Enterpayments-V1

Scenario: Visa Electron, UK, over 50
  Given the card is 4218 9303 0309 3990
  And the amount is 100
  When the payment is made
  The selected gateway is RBS

....
```

The team that implemented the related story suffered from a ton of bugs and difficult maintenance, largely caused by the way they captured examples. A huge list such as this one is not easy to break into separate tasks. This means that only one pair of developers could work on it instead of sharing the load with others. Because of this, the initial implementation of underlying features took a few weeks. There was so much complexity in the scenarios, but nobody could say if they painted the complete picture. Because the list of scenarios was difficult to understand, automated tests did not give business users any confidence, and they had to spend time manually testing the story as well. The long list of scenarios gave the delivery team a false sense of completeness, so they did not discuss important boundary conditions with business stakeholders. Several important cases were interpreted by different people in different ways. This surfaced only after a few weeks of running in production.

Although each individual scenario might seem understandable, pages and pages of this sort of stuff make it hard to see the big picture. These examples try to show how to select a payment processor, but the rules aren't really clear from the examples. The objective was to send low-risk transactions to a cheaper processor, and high-risk transactions to a more expensive processor with better fraud controls.

An overly complex specification is often a sign that the technical model is misaligned with the business model, or that the specification is described at the wrong level of abstraction. Even when correctly understood, such specifications lead to software that is hard to maintain, because small changes in the business environment can lead to disproportionately huge changes in the software.

For example, important business concepts such as transaction risk, processing cost or fraud capabilities were not captured in the examples for payment routing. Because of this, small changes to the business rules required huge changes to a complex network of special cases in the software. Minor adjustments to risk thresholds led to a ton of unexpected consequences. When one of the processors with good fraud-control capabilities reduced prices, most of the examples had to change and the underlying functions were difficult to adjust. That means that the organisation couldn't take advantage of the new business opportunity quickly.

Instead of capturing complex scenarios, it is far better to focus on illustrating user stories with key examples. Key examples are a small number of relatively simple scenarios that are easy to understand, evaluate for completeness and critique. This doesn't mean throwing away precision – quite the opposite – it means finding the right level of abstraction and the right mental model that can describe a complex situation better.

The payment routing case could be broken down into several groups of smaller examples. One group would show transaction risk based on the country of residence and country of purchase. Another group of examples would describe how to score transactions based on payment amount and currency. Several more groups of examples would describe other transaction scoring rules, focused only on the relevant characteristics. One overall set of examples would describe how to combine different scores, regardless of how they were calculated.

A final group of examples would describe how to match the risk score with compatible payment processors, based on processing cost and fraud capabilities. Each of these groups might have five to ten important examples. Individual groups would be much easier to understand. Taken together, these key examples would allow the team to describe the same set of rules much more precisely but with far fewer examples than before.

Key benefits

Several simple groups of key examples are much easier to understand and implement than a huge list of complex scenarios. With hundreds of examples, it's impossible to know if we need to add another one or not. Smaller groups make it easier to evaluate completeness and argue about boundary conditions, so they allow teams to discover and resolve inconsistencies and differences in understanding.

Breaking down complex examples into several smaller and focused groups leads to more modular software. If the transaction risk was modelled with examples of individual scoring rules, that would give a strong hint to the delivery team to capture those rules as separate functions. Changes to an individual scoring threshold would not impact all the other rules. This would avoid unexpected consequences when rules change. Changing the preferred processor when they reduce prices would require small localised changes instead of causing weeks of confusion.

Describing different aspects of a story with smaller and focused groups of key examples allows teams to divide work better. Two people can take the country-based scoring rules, two other people could implement routing based on final score. Smaller groups of examples also become a natural way of slicing the story – some more complex rules could be postponed for a future iteration, but a basic set of rules could be deployed in a week and provide some useful business value.

Finally, focusing on key examples significantly reduces the sheer volume of scenarios that need to be checked. Assuming that there are six or seven different scoring rules and that each has five key examples, the entire process can be described with roughly eighty thousand examples (five to the power of seven). Breaking it down into groups would allow us to describe the same concepts with forty or so examples (five times seven, plus a few overall examples to show that the rules are connected correctly). This significantly reduces the time required to describe and discuss the examples. It also makes the testing much faster, whether it was automated or manual. Clearer coverage of examples and models also provide a much better starting point for any further exploratory testing.

How to make it work

The most important thing to remember is that if the examples are too complex, your work on refining a story isn't complete. There are many good strategies for dealing with complexity. Here are four techniques that we often use:

- Look for missing concepts
- Group by commonality and focus only on variations
- Split validation and processing
- Summarise and explore important boundaries

Overly complex examples, or too many examples, are often a sign that some important business concepts are not explicitly described. In the payment routing examples, transaction risk is implied but not explicitly described. Similarly, processor compatibility with card types is hiden inside lower level information. Discovering these concepts allows teams to offer alternative models and break down both the specification and the overall story into more manageable chunks. We can use one set of examples to describe how to calculate the risk score, and another for how to use a score once it is calculated.

Avoid mixing validation and usage. This is a common way of hiding business concepts. For example, teams often use the same set of examples to describe how to process a transaction and all the ways to reject a transaction without processing (card number in incorrect format, invalid card type based on first set of digits, incomplete user information etc). The hidden business concept in that case is 'valid transaction'. Making this explicit would allow splitting a single large set of complex examples into two groups – determining whether a transaction is valid, and working with a valid transaction. These groups can then be broken down further based on structure.

Long lists of examples often contain groups that are similar in structure or have similar values. In the payment routing story, there were several pages of scenarios with card numbers and country of purchase, a cluster of examples involving two countries (residence and delivery), and some scenarios where the value of a transaction was important. Identifying commonalities in structure is often a valuable first step for discovering meaningful groups. Each group can then be restructured to show only the important differences between examples, reducing the cognitive load.

The fourth good strategy is to identify important boundary conditions and focus on them, ignoring examples that do not increase our understanding. For example, if 50 USD is the risk threshold for low-risk countries, and 25 USD for high-risk countries, then the important boundaries are:

- 24.99 USD from a high-risk country
- 25 USD from a high-risk country
- 25 USD from a low-risk country
- 49.99 USD from a low-risk country
- 50 USD from a low-risk country

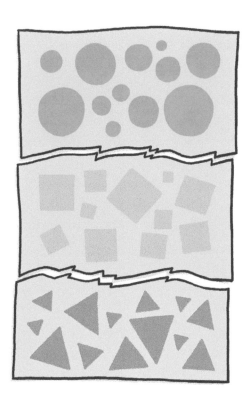

A major problem causing overly complex examples is the misunderstanding that testing can somehow be completely replaced by a set of carefully chosen examples. For most situations we've seen, this is a false premise. Checking examples can be a good start, but there are still plenty of other types of tests that are useful to do.

Don't aim to fully replace all testing activities for a user story with examples – aim to create a good shared understanding between team members and stakeholders, and give people the context to do a good job. Five examples that are easy to understand and at the right level of abstraction are much more effective for this than hundreds of very complex test cases.

CONTRAST EXAMPLES WITH COUNTER-EXAMPLES

Specification by example requires us to collaboratively discuss and explore the key examples that demonstrate how a desired feature should behave in different scenarios. The examples we choose are extremely important, as they must demonstrate the essence of the business rules of the feature. However, no matter how accurate or appropriate our examples, they will become more powerful and more valuable if supported by counter-examples.

Counter-examples are cases that show when the feature does not apply, or when the new behaviour is not invoked. In a test for a free delivery feature, we would of course expect to see examples of shopping scenarios where a customer order is eligible for free delivery. Counter-examples, on the other hand, would show important scenarios where the order is not eligible for free delivery.

Testers sometimes call these cases 'negative tests'. We tend to avoid that terminology as it devalues the importance of such scenarios. The reason counter-examples are so valuable is that they provide contrast.

Key benefits

What makes something stand out visually is the sharpness of the contrast against its background. But this does not mean that counter-examples should be wildly different from the key examples. In fact, good counter-examples are those where the inputs are as close as possible to the positive cases, but lead to different outputs. In general, we should use a set of counter-examples for each key example, where each counter-example highlights a different contributing factor or parameter that affects the rule.

Let's illustrate this with a free delivery example. The business rule for our new free delivery feature is as follows:

    Free delivery is offered to VIP customers who
    order five or more books in a single order.

The first key example to support this rule would probably be:

    An order of five books from a VIP customer
    qualifies for free delivery.

This is arguably the most concise example of the business rule, but on its own it would not give us confidence that we have a specification by example of the free delivery feature. Nor would we accept the feature if this was the only case that was checked against the implementation. To be confident that we offer free delivery if and only if the required criteria are met, we need to check some example cases where we do not offer free delivery.

To do so, we take the variables that affect the rule, and modify the value of just one at a time. We take quantity first. Hence:

```
An order of four books from a VIP customer does
not qualify for free delivery.
```

We can do the same for customer status:

```
An order of five books from a standard customer
does not qualify for free delivery.
```

Is that all that affects the rule? We mention books in the definition, but we also sell larger items that might be expensive to deliver. Examples allow us to be explicit about the status of orders like this:

```
An order of five refrigerators from a VIP
customer does not qualify for free delivery.
```

```
An order of five books and one refrigerator
from a VIP customer does not qualify for free
delivery.
```

How to make it work

Here's a sequence that might help you get started. Try it first by following each step. Once the idea of thinking about examples and counter-examples becomes the norm in your team, you won't have to follow this sequence methodically, you will just tend to create tables naturally as part of your discussions.

1. Start with the simplest example you can think of that shows a scenario where the feature or business rule takes effect. Write the example so that it makes sense when read aloud. (For example, express this scenario in the 'Given, When, Then' format.) Always prefer actual values over generalisations unless the value is irrelevant to the rule.
2. Underline the parts of the example that are most relevant to the feature or rule. Make sure you distinguish between inputs (for example, customer type, item type, quantity) and outputs (for example, free delivery eligibility). Using the values you have underlined, create a table with column names for each input and each output.
3. Put the data values from the first example into the table, as the first row.
4. For each output, identify a different possible value this output could take. Create an example that shows how this output value arises, using the smallest variation of the input values. Put these values into the table.
5. Repeat steps 2 and 3 until you have examples that include at least one row for each valid combination of the outputs.

When exploring key examples and counter-examples to illustrate the business rules, we are often not clear about the rules until we have explored and critiqued several good examples. Agreeing on the examples often leads to the need to restate the rules, or at least express them in clearer terms. For example, after discussing the examples about refrigerators, we would probably want to modify the free delivery rule to say something like:

```
Orders that include items other than books do
not qualify for free delivery.
```

DESCRIBE WHAT, NOT HOW

By far the most common mistake inexperienced teams make when describing acceptance criteria for a story is to mix the mechanics of test execution with the purpose of the test. They try to describe what they want to test and how something will be tested all at once, and get lost very quickly. Here is a typical example of a description of how something is to be tested:

```
Scenario: basic scenario
    Given the user Mike logs on
    And the user clicks on "Deposit"
    And the page reloads
    Then the page is "Deposit"
    And the user clicks on "10 USD"
    And the page reloads
    Then the page is "Card Payment"
    When the user enters a valid card number
    And the user clicks on "Submit"
    And the payment is approved
    And the page reloads
    Then the page is "Account"
    And the account field shows 10 USD
    And the user clicks on "Find tickets"
    And the user clicks on "Quick trip"
    And the page reloads
    Then the page is "Tickets"
    And the price is 7 USD
    And the user clicks on "Buy tickets"
    Then the purchase is approved
    And the page reloads
    And a ticket confirmation number is displayed
    And the account field shows 3 USD
```

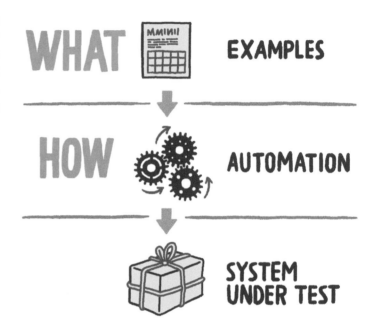

This is a good test only in the sense that someone with half a brain can follow the steps mechanically and check whether the end result is 3 USD. It is not a particularly useful test, because it hides the purpose in all the clicks and reloads, and leaves the team with only one choice for validating the story. Even if only a tiny fraction of the code contains most of the risk for this scenario, it's impossible to narrow down the execution. Every time we need to run the test, it will have to involve the entire end-to-end application stack. Such tests unnecessarily slow down validation and make automation more expensive. An even worse problem is that specifying acceptance criteria like this pretty much defeats the point of user stories – to have a useful conversation. This level of detail is too low to keep people interested in discussing the underlying assumptions.

Avoid describing the mechanics of test execution or implementation details with user stories. Don't describe how you will be testing something, keep the discussion focused on what you want to test instead. For example:

```
Scenario: pre-paid account purchases
Given a user with 10 USD in a pre-paid account
When the user attempts to buy a 7 USD ticket
Then the purchase is approved
And the user is left with 3 USD in the account
```

When most of the clutter is gone, it's easier to discuss more examples. For example, what if there is not enough money in the account?

Pre-paid balance	10 USD	5 USD
Ticket cost	7 USD	7 USD
Purchase status	approved	rejected
Resulting balance	3 USD	5 USD

This is where the really interesting part comes in. Once we remove the noise, it's easy to spot interesting boundaries and discuss them. For example, what if the pre-paid balance is 6.99 and someone wants to buy a 7 USD ticket?

As an experiment, go and talk to someone in sales about that case – most likely they'll tell you that you should take the customer's money. Talk to a developer, and most likely they'll tell you that the purchase should be rejected. Such discussions are impossible to have when the difficult decisions are hidden behind clicks, page loads and technical actions.

Key benefits

It's much faster to discuss what needs to be done instead of how it will be tested in detail, so keeping the discussion on a higher level allows the team to go through more stories faster, or in more depth. This is particularly important for teams that have limited access to business sponsors, and need to use their time effectively to make critical decisions.

Separately describing the purpose and the mechanics of a test makes it easier to use tests for communication and documentation. The next time a team needs to discuss purchase approval rules with business stakeholders, such tests will be a great help. Although the mechanics of testing will probably be irrelevant, a clear description of what the current system does will be an excellent start for the discussion. It will help to remind the team of all the difficult business decisions that were made months ago while working on previous stories. An acceptance criterion that mixes clicks and page loads with business decisions is useless for this.

Decoupling how something will be tested from what is being tested significantly reduces test maintenance costs. When a link on a web page becomes a button, or users are required to log in before opening a shopping cart, we only have to update the mechanics of testing. If the purpose and the mechanics are mixed together, it is impossible to identify what needs to change.

How to make it work

A good rule of thumb is to split the discussions on how and what into two separate meetings. Business sponsors are most likely not interested in the mechanics of testing, but they need to make decisions such as the $6.99 purchase. Engage decision-makers in whiteboard discussions on what needs to be tested, and postpone the other discussion.

If your team uses a tool to capture specifications with examples, such as Cucumber, FitNesse or Concordion, keep the human-readable level focused on what needs to be tested, and keep the automation level focused on how you're checking the examples. If you use something else, then clearly divide the purpose of the test and the mechanics of execution into different layers.

AVOID MATHEMATICAL FORMULAS

One typical way to waste time when specifying acceptance criteria through examples is to use mathematical formulas to describe categories of scenarios. This is a common beginner's mistake, and often comes from business stakeholders or analysts who are told that they need to provide examples with stories. By including mathematical formulas, people follow the form, but lose the substance. Here is an example we had recently with a reporting system:

```
Include all transactions in the thirty day period
before the report date.

Transaction date                          report?
-------------------------------------------------
Report date - 30 < Transaction            exclude
Report date - 30 < Transaction < Report date include
Transaction > Report date                 exclude
```

At first glance, this looks simple and complete. What could possibly go wrong with it?

The key issue with such examples expressed as formulas is that they effectively just restate the rules already specified somewhere else. The examples in the table only repeat the same information that we already have in the header sentence, and they do not communicate any more knowledge. We would have the same information even without the table. The examples do not provide any better structure for evaluating missing cases, measuring shared understanding or spotting potential mistakes. Even worse, examples such as these provide a false sense of completeness but can still hide quite a few questionable assumptions.

First of all, the data types aren't clear. Are both the report date and the transaction date only dates, or do they include time as well? Are time zones important? What happens at the boundaries? Should we include the transactions that took place on the report date, or exactly 30 days before the report date? If the data types are different, for example if the transaction date is actually a millisecond-accurate timestamp and the report date is a calendar date, should the transaction that happened at 00:01 on 3/3/2015 be included in the report for 3/3/2015? Or do we only include transactions that took place up to midnight that day? Or just the ones until 23:59:59 the day before? If the report date is a timestamp, what happens during leap hours or at daylight saving time change boundaries?

As much as possible, avoid using mathematical formulas in scenarios. In particular, avoid selecting equivalence classes for parameters or inputs based on formulas. Make the scenarios more precise by listing actual values, and try to provide representative examples for such values.

Key benefits

Concrete examples make it much easier to discuss boundaries, compared to examples specified using abstract mathematical formulas. A real timestamp makes it obvious that we need to consider minutes or even milliseconds when looking at edge cases. Adding or removing time zone information to the examples prompts people to ask about global or local execution, and how to do comparisons in the case of daylight time saving changes.

Real examples make it much more difficult to hide assumptions. A few concrete dates in the table would prompt someone to ask questions about boundaries, what happens when the transaction date and the report date are the same, and what does it mean for them to be same. This will help teams discuss and discover requirements before delivery.

How to make it work

Avoid specifying input equivalence classes using intervals or formulas. Insist on concrete examples around the relevant boundaries instead. Examples with formulas might be a nice start for the discussion, but transform each formula into at least two concrete boundaries as a group once the discussion starts. The problem with formulas is mostly related to inputs. Ranges and intervals are OK for output equivalence classes, for example with non-deterministic processes where acceptable values can have a margin of error.

Sometimes people write formulas or intervals because it's not clear why certain concrete values indicate important boundaries. For example, if we just used a transaction at 29:59:59.999 on 3/3/2015 for a report executed on 3 April, the complexity of the time-stamp value might confuse readers, and it may not be immediately obvious why that particular value was chosen. In cases such as this, it's perfectly fine to add a comment or a description next to the example – even if it's specified as an interval or a formula. But it's critical to also include a concrete example, and use that to automate testing.

To avoid a more general related problem, evaluate examples and scenarios and check whether they simply restate the knowledge you already have from the contextual description or the title of the test. Do your examples make things more concrete, or just repeat the information you already have? Unless examples are making things more concrete, they will mislead people into a false assumption of completeness, so they need to be restated.

Choosing a representative example for a whole class of items is one of the key techniques for good test design, and most people understand it intuitively. For example, if we're exploring an application that allows users to log in through external identity providers, we'd check it with one Google account, one Facebook account and one Twitter account. Unless there is some very compelling reason that would make one Google account significantly different from another, we wouldn't try the same tests with additional Google e-mails. That would be a waste of time. However, this intuitive approach can also be quite misleading.

Teams often apply equivalence class reduction only to inputs, which can result in a false assumption of completeness. There are two sides to explore for equivalence class design: inputs and outputs. Choosing the wrong set can easily deceive teams into thinking that the system has been thoroughly tested, when in fact serious problems are hiding. This is particularly problematic when describing actions with several types of outputs.

For example, validation messages are just another output type, but they are rarely considered as important as the primary workflow. As a really simplistic illustration, several invalid combinations of usernames and email addresses could all be classified as equivalent from the input perspective in a user registration scenario, but they might be importantly different from the output perspective. An attempt to register with empty username and email address should definitely fail, and we can check that the registration was rejected. However, this does not prove that validation works. Validation errors in one field can mask or hide validation errors in another field. Email address validation might be completely broken, yet the action would have been rejected just because of the username, or the other way around. To really de-risk this action, we have to check lots of different combinations of valid and invalid usernames and email addresss. These are all equivalent from the input perspective (all invalid), but significantly different from the output perspective, since validation errors are also outputs.

If the activity you're describing has several types of outputs, make sure that you explore equivalence classes for all of them.

Key benefits

Evaluating different perspectives for equivalence classes provides better conceptual test coverage, while still keeping the number of examples that need to be tested relatively small. It's a good way of avoiding tunnel vision and preventing rare but catastrophic failures.

Primary workflows and paths tend to be better explained and communicated, and teams pay more attention when implementing and checking them. But secondary outputs don't receive nearly as much attention. As a result, error handling procedures are often much weaker than the main thread of work. According to *CWE/SANS Top 25 Most Dangerous Software Errors*, the top four riskiest programming mistakes are caused by bad handling of invalid inputs.

Problems in secondary outputs tend to cascade and spread, causing other issues, so they are particularly troublesome. Yuan, Zhang, Rodrigues et al. suggest in *Analysis of Production Failures in Distributed Data-Intensive Systems* that stricter testing of error handling could have prevented several catastrophic failures at large online systems such as Amazon and Facebook.

Looking at different ways to slice equivalence classes can also open up a fruitful discussion on software design. For example, after exploring equivalence classes for secondary outputs, a team we worked with realised that they had similar auditing requirements for many of their workflows. Before that, each workflow duplicated auditing procedures and there was a lot of inconsistency in audit trail handling. Once the team noticed the similarities, they created a common auditing module, and engaged their business stakeholders in a discussion on auditing needs. This removed a lot of unnecessary code, reduced future maintenance costs and allowed the team to bring in new features faster. In addition, it provided business stakeholders with a consistent and direct access to all audit trail activities.

How to make it work

To make sure all perspectives are considered, experiment with splitting into groups when you design equivalence classes, and get one group to focus on inputs, and another on outputs. This often leads to useful discussions when the groups come back together.

A useful reminder is to explore input equivalence for processing valid cases, and output equivalence for processing invalid cases. Bach, Caner and Pettichord call this heuristic 'Test Every Error Message' in *Lessons Learned in Software Testing*. However, consider this as part of a more general rule. There are many other types of secondary outputs that teams often do not think about. Common examples are audit trails, archive logs, alerts and post-processing tasks.

CLEARLY SEPARATE INPUTS AND OUTPUTS

In *Fifty Quick Ideas To Improve Your User Stories*, we recommended not getting too stuck on format consistency. User stories are all about facilitating fruitful discussions. In order to achieve this, it's better to be flexible and not enforce a particular structure or format of story cards. The same holds for story conversations, enforcing a particular format or tool is not effective. But the third aspect of good stories – the confirmation criteria – does not follow the same pattern. Good structure and strict rules on formatting are quite beneficial here.

Inexperienced teams often mess up the acceptance criteria by mixing up information in an unstructured way, so that it is unclear what is actually being checked. Here's a typical example:

```
Scenario: New user, suspicious transaction

Given a user registered from UK
And the user completes a 60 USD order
And asks for delivery to US
Then the transaction is marked as suspicious
```

```
When the order completes
And the user places a 30 USD order
And asks for delivery to UK
Then the transaction is marked as checked

When the order completes
And the user places a 30 USD order
And asks for delivery to US
Then the transaction is marked as checked
```

Try to read through the example and work out what causes transactions to be marked as suspicious. Is it the amount? Is it the country of registration being different than the delivery country? What's the purpose of the third example and how is it different from the first one? Is there a difference between 'the user completes an order' in the first example and 'the user places an order' in the second and third examples?

Acceptance criteria for stories are pretty useless if people can't quickly understand their purpose. The previous example comes from a delivery system, where orders are suspicious if the delivery country differs from the country of registration, unless the address was previously used for an approved order. Is that what you guessed? The amount is pretty irrelevant, and the address is not captured in the examples. It was hidden in the configuration of test automation.

Scenarios with unclear structure are misleading. They just cause problems. People can easily understand them differently. Someone can implement the story and make the tests pass, while completely missing the point and introducing lots of bugs. If the suspicious transaction scenario is automated as a test, it will be difficult to understand what was covered in automation and what was left for testers to check manually, and it won't be easy to figure out good variables for exploratory testing either. Enforcing a strict structure is a good way to prevent such issues.

Another typical example of bad test structure is an output or assertion without any clear inputs. It's easy to spot these when the acceptance criterion only has a wireframe or a report screenshot, with an assumption to 'test it is like this'. That is not a useful criterion unless we know under which conditions. And before someone says 'always', look at some input fields on the wireframe and ask questions. What happens if the content is too long? What if it starts scrolling? What if there are more than two pictures? Assumptions about something always happening are frequently wrong.

One of the best ways of untangling messy scenarios is to separate inputs and outputs.

Key benefits

An acceptance criterion where inputs and outputs are clearly separated is much easier to understand than scenarios of interleaved information without context. This makes people think about what they really need to set up, what needs to be evaluated, and

often eliminates a lot of unnecessary detail. In addition, it helps teams to spot gaps and inconsistencies more easily. If the specification of acceptance is easier to understand, it is easier to check for completeness, easier to implement and easier to verify.

A clear structure is also a better starting point for both test automation and exploratory testing. Well-structured examples make it easier to see where to put in automation hooks. Clearly separated inputs also make it easy to think about experiments with those values, and identify any boundary conditions that have not been covered. Once the inputs are identified, experimenting with inputs can help to uncover those fake assumptions about something always happening.

How to make it work

For information captured in tables, it's good to pull inputs to the left and keep outputs on the right. Most people find this organisation intuitive. It's then easy to see if all examples have some common input values, and make tables even smaller by pulling values into a background or a set-up section.

For information captured in sentences or bullet points, put inputs at the top and outputs at the bottom. If you're using one of the tools where examples are described as given-when-then, this translates to putting the 'given' statements at the top, and 'then' statements at the bottom of your scenarios. Ideally, have only one 'when' statement – that's the action under test.

If you have a messy scenario, don't spend a lot of time cleaning it up. If it's proving to be difficult to separate inputs and outputs, that's a huge warning sign that the team doesn't understand the story completely. Instead of wasting time on cleaning up the test, organise another discussion about the story and write some better examples.

ASK 'WHAT HAPPENS INSTEAD?'

Testing asynchronous systems is never easy, but proving that something does not happen in an asynchronous system is often a tall order even for the best teams. For example, if a user account does not contain enough money for a transaction to be applied, it's easy to check that an error message was presented to the user, but much harder to check that some background process did not capture the transaction. There is always a risk that we're not looking in the right place, that we're declaring success too soon, or that the process had an unexpected side effect. To add insult to injury, tests that need to prove that something did not happen often deal with validation constraints and error cases, which means that side effects are even more dangerous.

Waiting for an event instead of waiting for a period of time is the preferred way of testing asynchronous systems, but when you need to check that something does not happen, there is no event to wait for. The only option is to wait for some arbitrary period of time. Such tests are brittle, environment-dependent, and easily affected by many other factors (for example, a different test running on the same environment that can log a similar transaction and confuse everything). The problem is compounded by the fact that testing that something does not happen often involves invalid data, and thus there is no unique identifier to validate against data sources, so the checks have to process a lot of information, making them even slower.

DESIGNING GOOD CHECKS

A good solution for such situations is to ask 'what happens instead?' and validate the resulting condition. For example, instead of checking that a transaction does not exist after a period of time, check that a failed transaction was logged in an audit trail. For even better risk coverage, validate that the transaction was not processed immediately afterwards.

Ideally, the alternative event should become observable at the same time that the original event would normally happen. For example, the audit log record is generated by the same back-end code that processes transactions. This makes it easy to be confident that there will be no further processing for that particular test case.

Key benefits

Describing an alternative event instead of the absence of an event makes a test more reliable, because we can wait until an event happens instead of just waiting for a period of time. It removes potential interference from other tests, because each test can work with a unique identifier.

However, the biggest advantage of this approach is actually not in improving testablity, but in discovering additional assumptions and hidden requirements. For example, instead of just ignoring failed log-in attempts, we could log them for later analysis. Spotting unusual data patterns or spikes in failed log-ins might help us to detect unauthorised access attempts early, and make the system more secure by introducing additional rules. With regard to this particular situation, one of the teams we worked with discussed it with their security specialists, and decided that any user account with more than five unsuccessful log-in attempts in one hour should be temporarily blocked and flagged for manual investigation. This allowed security experts to spot patterns and prevent future hacking attempts easier.

How to make it work

The best time to enquire about alternative events is during a discussion about a user story, to ensure that genuine business requirements for auditing or traceability don't go unnoticed. Sometimes, the discussion about what should happen instead can lead you to discover a completely different set of requirements. For example, when a team at one of our clients were discussing how to route payment requests, they couldn't agree about what to do with foreign currency transactions. They originally envisaged handling only single currency transaction requests, but the developers pointed out that the external API they planned to use could potentially send transactions in different currencies. It was clear that such transactions shouldn't be processed directly, but stakeholders had completely different ideas about what to do instead. Some people argued that they should be rejected, some people argued that they should be converted to the primary currency and processed, and some people argued that although the external API supported transactions in foreign currencies, their customers would never use anything other than the primary currency. In situations such as this, it's often best to split out the alternative scenario into a different user story. In this case, we agreed that foreign currency transactions should go to a manual payment list, and that we would let stakeholders decide what to do about them on a case-by-case basis until they could come up with a more general solution.

If there is no business-domain requirement to add an audit trail or an alternative event, consider using log files or some other technical output to detect the end of asynchronous processing. A good trick is to assign some kind of unique identifier to the asynchronous request, and then wait during testing until the log file or some error queue contains an element with that identifier.

USE GIVEN-WHEN-THEN IN A STRICT SEQUENCE

Given-When-Then seems to be the de-facto standard for expressing functional checks using examples. Introduced as part of JBehave in 2003, this structure was intended to support conversations between teams and business stakeholders, but also lead those discussions towards a conclusion that would be easy to automate as a test.

Given-When-Then statements are great because they are easy to capture on whiteboards and flipcharts, and also easy to transfer to electronic documents, including plain text files and wiki pages. In addition, there are automation tools for all popular application platforms today that support tests specified as Given-When-Then.

On the other hand, Given-When-Then is a very sharp tool and unless handled properly, it can hurt badly. Without understanding the true purpose of the format, many teams follow the form but create tests that are too long, too difficult to maintain, and almost impossible to understand. Here is a typical example:

```
Scenario: Payroll salary calculations

Given the admin page is open
When the user selects 'employee admin'
Given the user types John into the 'name'
and the user types 30000 into the 'salary'
and the user clicks 'Add'
Then the page reloads
When the user selects 'employee admin'
And the user types Mike into the 'name'
and the user types 40000 into the 'salary'
and the user clicks 'Add'
Then the user selects 'Payslips'
Given the user selects employee number 1
Then the user clicks on 'View'
When the user selects 'Info'
Then the 'salary' shows 29000
Then the user clicks 'Edit'
and the user types 40000 into the 'salary'
When the user clicks on 'View'
And the 'salary' shows 31000
```

This example might have been clear to the person who first wrote it, but its purpose is unclear – what is it really testing? Is the salary amount a parameter of the test, or is it an expected outcome? If one of the later steps of this scenario fails, it will be very difficult to understand the exact cause of the problem.

Spoken language is ambiguous, and it's perfectly OK to say 'Given an employee has a salary ..., When the tax deduction is..., then the employee gets a payslip and the payslip shows ...'. It's also OK to say 'When an employee has a salary ..., Given the tax deduction is ...' or 'Given an employee ... and the tax deduction ... then the payslip ...'. All those combinations mean the same thing, and they can easily be understood within the wider context.

But there is only one right way to describe this situation with Given-When-Then, at least if you want to get the most out of it from the perspective of long-term test maintenance.

Given-When-Then is not just an automation-friendly way of describing expectations, it's a structural pattern for designing clear specifications. It's been around for quite a while under different names. When use cases were popular, it was known as Preconditions-Trigger-Postconditions. In unit testing, it's known as Arrange-Act-Assert. Effectively, all those names mean the same thing: make sure that actions, parameters and outputs are not mixed together.

The sequence is important: 'Given' comes before 'When', and 'When' comes before 'Then'. Those clauses should not be mixed. All parameters should be specified with 'Given' clauses, the action under test should be specified with the 'When' clause, and all expected outcomes should be listed with 'Then' clauses. Each scenario should ideally have only one 'When' clause that clearly points to the purpose of the test.

Key benefits

Using Given-When-Then in sequence reminds people very effectively about several great ideas for test design:

- It suggests that preconditions and postconditions need to be identified and separated (see the section *Clearly separate inputs and outputs* for more information).
- It suggests that the purpose of the test should be clearly communicated, and that each scenario should check one and only one thing (see the section *One test, one topic*).
- When there is only one action under test, people are forced to look beyond the mechanics of test execution and really identify a clear purpose (see the section *Describe what, not how*).

When used correctly, Given-When-Then helps teams design specifications and checks that are easy to understand and maintain. As tests are focused on one particular action, they are less brittle and easier to diagnose and troubleshoot. When the parameters and expectations are clearly separated, it's easier to evaluate whether we need to add more examples, and

How to make it work

A good trick that prevents most accidental misuses of Given-When-Then is to use past tense for 'Given' clauses, present tense for 'When' and future tense for 'Then'. This makes it clear that 'Given' statements are preconditions and parameters, and that 'Then' statements are postconditions and expectations.

Make 'Given' and 'Then' passive – they should describe values rather than actions. Make sure 'When' is active – it should describe the action under test.

ONE TEST, ONE TOPIC

Lack of focus is a symptom of problematic tests that is relatively easy to spot. Common examples of lack of focus are multiple actions that are covered by a single test and sequences of actions that are executed multiple times with slightly different parameters. In the Given-When-Then structure of examples, this symptom translates to multiple 'When' statements, or a single 'When' statement that uses conjunctions.

If a test executes multiple tasks that together create a higher-level action, it is often a sign that it is tightly coupled to a particular technical workflow. Such tests are often written after development and rely on implementation details, which makes them fragile. Here is a typical example:

```
When the user submits the payment details
And the admin approves the payment
And the payment is scheduled
And the payment is executed by the channel
And the payment is sent to the counterparty
And the payment confirmation arrives
And the payment confirmation is loaded
```

This example lists individual steps that happen in a particular implementation that has two asynchronous modules. If the way technical components are coordinated changes in the future, the test will break even if none of the business rules change, nor the software implementation of payment processing. A particularly problematic category of such tests are those where tasks or actions rely on user interface details.

A test that executes multiple interdependent actions is fragile and often costs a lot to maintain. Actions within a sequence depend on the results of preceding actions, so small changes in one such action can cause fake alerts and failures in the expectations for other actions. Such tests are difficult to troubleshoot and fix, because interdependencies make it difficult to understand and change expectations correctly.

Each test should ideally be focused on one topic. Each topic should ideally described by one test. Watch out for multiple 'When' clauses, actions with conjunctions and scenario names that suggest a lack of focus. Break them down into several independent tests, and you will get a lot more value out of them.

Key benefits

Several independent tests for different actions are much easier to maintain than one overall test that validates everything. When one of the actions changes, it is easier to understand the impact on the test and adjust expectations, because the impact is localised. Similarly, changes to tests for one action do not require changes to tests for other actions, but this is impossible to prevent with a single overarching test.

When tests are focused on one particular action, it's easier to argue about completeness and add more contextual examples around important boundary conditions for that particular action. Tests that execute multiple actions suffer from a combinatorial explosion of potential boundary conditions, so they often just check one scenario rather than exploring important boundaries.

Independent tests also allow faster feedback. When developers work on one of the actions, they can run only the specific tests for that action instead of waiting for the other actions to complete as well.

How to make it work

There are several good strategies for cleaning up tests that execute multiple actions, depending on the dependencies between the actions.

If a test executes multiple tasks in sequence that form a higher-level action, often the language and the concepts used in the test explain the mechanics of test execution rather than the purpose of the test, and in this case the entire block can often be replaced with a single higher-level concept. Here is an example:

```
When the payroll is submitted for approval
And the payroll is approved
And the payments are queued
And the payslips are generated
And employees receive the payment
```

If the individual steps show important preconditions, and for example we want to test what happens if the payments are not queued, such conditions should move to a 'Given' clause rather than staying in a 'When' clause. See the section *Use Given-When-Then in a strict sequence* for more information.

If the individual steps do not demonstrate important variations, but are executed in sequence just because of the technical flow of implementation, then the entire block can be replaced by a single higher-level action, such as:

```
When the payroll is processed
```

See the section on *Specify what, Not how* for some ideas on how to deal with such cases.

If a test executes interdependent actions because they have similar inputs and reuse outputs, it's best to split them into individual scenarios. A good technique for this is to:

1. Group all common parameters into a single set-up block (in the Given-When-Then structure this would normally go into a common Background section).
2. Build a separate scenario for each 'When' clause, listing all individual parameters required for it directly. Avoid any actions in the 'Given' clause, instead specify the preconditions as values
3. Split the 'Then' clauses of the original test and assign them to the relevant focused scenario.
4. Evaluate scenarios without a 'Then' clause, because they do not actually check anything. If they were there just to set up the context for some other scenario, delete them. If they describe an important aspect of the system, add the relevant expectations.

TREAT TOO MANY BOUNDARIES AS A MODELLING PROBLEM

Complex models are difficult to describe. Even when the general cases of such models can be easily understood, they typically imply a vast number of boundary conditions and special cases.

By implication, software systems built to automate such models are also very difficult to test. Related edge cases needing tests are often captured using huge state-transition tables, complex state diagrams or a combinatorial explosion of input and output examples. It's almost impossible to know if anyone has a complete picture with such complex models, so it is also difficult to decide how much testing is enough. Tests with too many edge cases are difficult to understand and difficult to update. They are often also very brittle, so they will be costly to maintain.

There are several popular techniques for managing and designing tests for such situations, such as pairwise testing and path-based coverage, but in many situations they are actually solving the wrong problem.

Difficult testing is a symptom, not a problem. When it is difficult for a team to know if they have a complete

picture during testing, then it will also be difficult for it to know if they have a complete picture during development, or during a discussion on requirements. It's unfortunate that this complexity sometimes clearly shows for the first time during testing, but the cause of the problem is somewhere else.

It's more useful to think about this as a modelling problem, not a testing problem. A huge number of special cases and boundary conditions often means that the team chose wrong concepts and abstractions for the underlying software model, or that parts of the system are too tightly coupled to be considered in isolation. This might also mean that the software system is not well aligned with the processes it's trying to automate, or problems it's trying to solve.

For example, a team at a financial trading company we worked with was re-writing their accounting and reporting system. Reporting regulations and tax rules differ from country to country, so their initial testing ideas resulted in several whiteboards full of difficult boundary conditions. Even when they ran out of wall space to write examples, it was clear to everyone that this was only the tip of the iceberg. It would be easy to explain this situation as a testing issue, caused by a complex domain and a complex organisational structure. Teams in large companies tend to think that their domains are much more complex than other software, and accept difficult testing as a fact of life. However, that is often a self-fulfilling prophecy. Because people accept overly-complex solutions, testing becomes expensive and complex, making it more difficult to clean up the design. Looking at this as a modelling problem, not as a testing problem, the team discovered several missing domain concepts, such as an abstraction of the 'trade origin'. They broke down the test cases into those that help them calculate a trade origin, and those that use a trade origin, regardless of how it's calculated, to choose tax rules and reporting needs. This led to a much better designed system.

Key benefits

In the past, if people discovered that a software model was wrong during testing, it was too late to do anything useful. The people who designed test cases rarely had any say over software design models, and by the time testing started there was typically too much software written to change it fundamentally. However, with the ongoing trend towards shorter delivery phases and integrating testing and development, discovering an overly complex model during testing can be quite timely and useful. Instead of accepting the situation and trying to fight the large number of boundary conditions with test management techniques, teams can use this as a signal that they need to start remodelling the underlying system.

Treating too many boundary conditions as a signal that the model needs changing helps teams create better software architecture and design, which leads to systems that are much easier to test. Better decoupling between different components of the model leads to more focused test cases. By removing interdependencies, creating better interfaces and higher-level abstractions, we can avoid a combinatorial explosion of inputs and outputs, replacing large state-transition tables and complex diagrams with several isolated sets of focused key examples. This means that there are fewer test cases needed for the same risk coverage, so it is faster to check the system against such test cases, and easier and cheaper to maintain the tests.

However, the key benefit of better software models is not actually in easier testing – it's in easier evolution. By reducing the overall complexity of software models, we get systems that are easier to understand, so they will be easier to develop. They will also be cheaper to maintain, because changes will be better localised, and easier to extend because individual parts will be easier to replace.

How to make it work

Evaluate potential models by experimenting with test case design before programming. If the underlying model is difficult to describe with a relatively small number of key examples, try alternative models. In his book *Domain Driven Design*, Eric Evans argues that such situations are often caused by the mental models of business stakeholders and delivery teams being misaligned, and that looking for hidden or implied domain concepts generally leads to breakthroughs in design.

Don't immediately take the first idea for remodelling that comes along. Try three or four different approaches and compare them to see which one leads to fewer scenarios and clearer structure for examples.

PREFER SMALLER TABLES

A specification with examples often collects sets of key examples into tables, to show clearly how different inputs lead to different outputs. The power of tables is that they reduce a problem to the key relationships that matter, and remove as much semantic noise as possible. But depending on the number of rules, exceptions and nuances that affect the feature being specified, these tables of examples can grow quite large. This is a problem, as it detracts from the usefulness of the table form. We want tables to clarify our examples, not hide them, and for this purpose smaller tables tend to be more effective than larger ones.

A common cause of oversized tables is that people try to use a single, large table to illustrate too many different aspects of a feature. In any given specification, there may be many dependent variables, each one becoming a new column in a wider and wider table. As the number of columns grows, the more possible combinations of values need to be covered, leading to an explosion of rows of examples.

Let's take a blackjack game application as an example. The payout to a player depends on many factors, so to describe it we would need to specify the rules for how a player wins or loses and how much they get back on their bet. To cover these cases we might create a table that looks something like the one below. Even this large table does not explore all the interesting combinations of input values, and we would probably want more examples of each of the different results to understand them completely, so a table like this could easily grow much larger. Yet it is already too big to be expressive and useful as living documentation.

The best way to overcome this combinatorial explosion is to deal with one rule or concept at a time, and only include the subset of variables and example values that are relevant to it. Our feature specification would therefore consist of a set of connected concepts, each with small tables of examples to illustrate it.

The first six rows are basic cases, where the player takes no special action. Therefore we could have a separate simpler table for these examples. We can also separate the concept of result from that of payout, dealing with each separately. That means we can remove references to bets from our examples about determining the result.

bet	double	insure	surrender	player	dealer	result?	payout?
10	no	no	no	19	18	win	20
10	no	no	no	18	19	lose	0
10	no	no	no	19	19	push	10
10	no	no	no	BJ	19	blackjack	25
20	no	no	no	10	bust	win	40
10	no	no	no	bust	bust	lose	0
10	yes	no	no	19	18	win	40
10	no	no	yes	6	18	surrender	5
10	no	yes	no	21	BJ	lose	10
10	no	yes	no	21	19	win	20

After the simple cases, we can introduce the special cases of winning with a blackjack, and going bust.

player	dealer	result?
19	18	win
18	19	lose
19	19	push
BJ	19	blackjack
10	bust	win
bust	bust	lose

Having given several examples of what hand-value combinations lead to the different results, we can show the relationship between bets, results and payouts.

bet	result	payout?
10	win	20
20	win	40
10	blackjack	25
10	push	10
10	lose	0

Using the same strategy, we can create a separate table to illustrate the special case of insurance (similarly for doubling, splitting, and so on). We can fix the bet amount to 10 and only use columns specific to the insurance scenarios.

insured	player	dealer	payout?	ins. payout?
yes	21	BJ	0	15
no	21	BJ	0	0
yes	19	21	0	0
yes	BJ	BJ	10	15
yes	BJ	17	25	0

Key benefits

Smaller tables allow you to focus a set of related examples on a single rule (see also *One test, one topic*). You only need to include the columns and values that are relevant to that rule. Maintaining smaller tables is much easier, as a change to system behaviour is usually localised to the few tables that deal specifically with that behaviour.

Finding errors in the examples is much quicker when the relationship between the rules and their examples is clear, and this is easier with several smaller tables. For example, the ninth row of the first large table contains an error (total payout should be 15, not 10) but it is not obvious. That case is equivalent to the first row of the last table, where the mistake would be more apparent, especially if we precede the table with short rule descriptions, e.g. 'Insurance is a separate bet, for half the original bet value (i.e. 5 for a bet of 10). Insurance pays 2:1, if the dealer has a Blackjack.'

How to make it work

Start by breaking a table into groups of examples that are related to a single concept. You will improve readability just by having several tables each with a fewer number of rows.

In these smaller groups, look for columns that have the same value, or values that don't directly affect the outputs. Remove these columns.

Make sure each table has a brief text introduction to describe the concept or rule that the examples in the table illustrate. Link the related concepts and tables so that it is easy to navigate between related tables.

Behaviour-driven development (BDD) test artifacts and executable specifications should ideally be designed to serve three important roles:

- Specification (of what needs to be implemented or changed)
- Acceptance tests (for the specific cases to be checked as part of acceptance of this feature)
- Documentation (of the behaviour of this feature)

To get the most value out of all three roles, we need to find a balance between the 'three C's' of executable specifications:

- Conciseness (of specification)
- Completeness (of test coverage)
- Coherence (of documentation)

When creating your artifacts, remember the three roles they must serve at different times: now as a specification, soon as acceptance tests, and later as living documentation. Critique the artifact from each perspective. How well does it serve each distinct role? Is it over-optimised for one role to the detriment of others?

Key benefits

When we find the right balance between each of these forces (conciseness, completeness, coherence), one artifact serves all three purposes effectively. To succeed in this, we need to be clear and precise about the topic (this addresses conciseness) but draw attention to the important relationships and special cases as well as the norm (this satisfies completeness.) We also need to provide a context for the examples in the form of a well-written introduction and achieve a balance between general rules and specific examples (this addresses coherence).

A specification is optimal when it is as concise as possible. Such a concise specification avoids repetition, extraneous details, redundancy, and overlap with information contained in other related specifications. Conciseness helps an implementation team understand the exact scope of what must be implemented or changed, with the minimum distraction.

A suite of acceptance tests needs to be complete in terms of its coverage of the target feature and of other features with which it is integrated. The greater the coverage, the less the regression and integration risk for this story or feature. Good acceptance tests ensure that not just the 'happy path' is checked, but all alternative paths and dead ends too. This means that to avoid those it-fell-through-the-cracks types of defects, we tend to test beyond the edges of the feature or change – the test footprint is usually bigger than the change footprint. This in itself is not a bad thing, but this tendency is a force that competes directly with the need for conciseness for the sake of the specification. We also need to recognise that there are good test cases and not-so-good test cases, and we should not get carried away with trying to cover every possible case. Completeness therefore needs to be understood as an influencing force, but not an absolute goal.

Documentation needs to be coherent, meaning that each artifact is logical and understandable on its own, as well as consistent with others in its style and terminology. This coherence enhances shared understanding and reduces the cost of ownership of

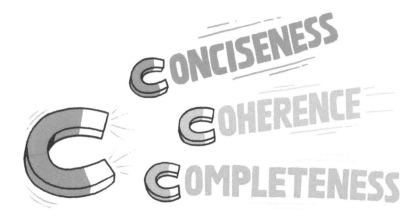

CONCISENESS
COHERENCE
COMPLETENESS

the product in the long term. It extends the valuable life of our specifications and tests, and represents a return on the investment we make in them. Coherence of documentation is also enhanced when we closely match our rule descriptions to the examples that illustrate them.

How to make it work

When teams capture details written on a whiteboard or similar media in a specification workshop, they typically have the key examples of cases and scenarios that were discussed to tease out the complexity of the business rules. The next step is to add enough context to these examples so that they will make sense to people who were not involved in the discussions that created them. In *User Story Mapping* Jeff Patton has described the artifacts we create in collaborative workshops as being like vacation photos, because they mean more to the people who were there when the photos were taken than to those who weren't. For those who took part in the specification workshop, the key examples they wrote down and still have are like snapshots that trigger memories of all the other things that happened at the time – the discussions, questions and answers, revisions and corrections that the group

went through together in the process of arriving at those examples. It is important to remember that we are trying to create items of long-term value. We need to build up the picture in a logical way, so that everyone can get the most value out of the specifications.

You will get the best results by thinking ahead to the longer term role of coherent documentation, rather than thinking only in terms of specifications or tests.

Here are some tips for doing this:

- Always provide some introductory text for each set of examples
- Show simple, illustrative examples before more complex ones
- Group small sets of related or complementary examples together
- Highlight your key examples and keep them prominent in your specifications, close to the descriptions of the business rules they illustrate
- If you also have a more comprehensive set of tests that cover additional cases, keep these in separate tables or scenarios, or consider putting them in a separate feature file or page, and tag them accordingly.

WRITE ASSERTIONS FIRST

Overcomplicated inputs and background sections are one of the most common problems with example-based specifications and tests. This is effectively the extreme opposite of the problems described in the section *Avoid mathematical formulas*. By trying to make things concrete enough and avoid hidden assumptions in inputs, many teams go too far and specify context information and aspects of parameters that are not particularly relevant for the purpose of the test. This often takes the shape of background sections that are too long and include too many contextual details.

For example, one of the teams we worked with recently was working on calculations of tax deductions for various payment operations, and all their tests started with setting up financial instruments, defining tax rules for different territories, setting up accounts with a lot of personal details related to account holders, creating a history of transactions to seed an account and then proceeding to the actual purpose of a test. In sixty or seventy lines of text, only the bottom five were actually directly relevant to the purpose of a test. Everything else was there because people thought it made things more concrete, or because the underlying data models required reference information. Without thinking clearly about what they actually wanted to test, the people who wrote such scenarios added everything they thought would be important.

This makes specifications overly complex, and it becomes very difficult to understand which of the input parameters actually control the actions under test. It's also difficult to break up such documents if they become too complex, because it's unclear which input sections need to be kept or rephrased for individual actions.

Although it's natural to think about writing documents from top to bottom, with tests it is actually better to start from the bottom. Write the outputs, the assertions and the checks first. Then try to explain how to get to those outputs. In the case of the given-when-then style of scenarios, this effectively means to write the 'then' clauses first. In case of tabular specifications, this effectively means to write the columns on the right first and fill them in with data that would be used to check the outcome of the tests.

Key benefits

Starting from the outputs makes it highly unlikely that a test will try to check many different things at once, as those different aspects will naturally be split into different outputs. Writing outputs first helps to enforce many other aspects of good test design, such as focusing on a single action in a test and balancing clarity and completeness.

When tests are written from the outputs towards the inputs and contextual information, people tend to leave out all the incidental detail. If something isn't directly leading to one of the outputs, it doesn't need to be in the list of inputs. Tests that are written bottom up, by doing the outputs first, tend to be shorter and more directly explain the purpose.

Finally, if such tests grow too big or become too complex to understand, they are much easier to split into several tests than the ones written by thinking about inputs first. When tests are written by listing outputs first, the rest of the document is naturally tied to output structures. It is obvious which parts of the inputs go with which sections of outputs, if we need to slice the outputs.

How to make it work

Try to use concrete values instead of general descriptions for outputs. The more concrete the outputs, the more difficult it is to hide wrong assumptions in the tests.

Don't mistake this idea for writing documents with a single pass, where you completely define the bottom part, and then proceed to the middle and the top parts. That's just not going to work. Although thinking about outputs first provides focus for the rest of the test, writing that way is counter-intuitive, so it is difficult to discover all the key examples in a single pass. Likewise, outputs and inputs often have different classes of equivalence, so we'll need to consider both to fully explore the problem space. This means that we'll only discover some classes of inputs after we have defined some initial inputs.

Please iterate through outputs and inputs instead of expecting to complete them in a single attempt. It's perfectly OK to alternate between refining outputs and refining inputs. Start with one class of outputs, and that will lead to a set of related inputs. Then think about further boundaries and more examples you'd like to include, which will lead to more outputs. Don't try to get all the outputs right immediately before proceeding with the inputs. In particular, interesting boundaries and edge cases only start coming out only when you have some concrete idea about the inputs, so doing just a single pass from bottom to top would not allow you to benefit from that kind of discovery.

SPLIT TECHNICAL AND BUSINESS CHECKS

Many user stories involve both technical and business-oriented requirements. For example, automating credit card charge notifications might have an impact on order management (business), and also require support for particular XML message formats and network communication protocols (technical). All these aspects are important and need to be tested, so they often get bundled into the same test or specification.

Mixing technical and business aspects in a single test gives teams the worst of both worlds. To validate business flows, such tests are typically automated around entire components or even systems, which is quite inefficient for checking technical boundaries and edge cases. Invalid XML messages and message retry policies do not really need such a huge area of coverage, and they could be validated within much smaller code units. Mixing the tests makes technical testing much slower and more complex than it needs to be.

Technical testing normally requires the use of technical concepts, such as nested structures, recursive pointers and unique identifiers. Such things can be easily described in programming languages, but are not easy to put into the kind of form that non-technical testing tools require. So teams have to make a trade-off between precision and readability. This leads to descriptions that are not really precise but also not exactly easy to read, such as tables within tables with named cell references. Long-term maintenance becomes a huge problem because of the lack of shared understanding. When a small technical change requires a review of the tests, business domain experts will be unable to provide good feedback.

Both the technical and the business aspects are important, and they both need to be tested, but teams will often get a lot more value out of two separate sets of tests rather than one mixed-role test.

Key benefits

Dividing a single overarching test into several smaller and more focused tests makes it much easier to understand and maintain all the test documents. Teams can keep tests for aspects that require business domain feedback in a human readable form, so domain experts can provide good feedback. Meanwhile, they can use programming language constructs such as nested structures to describe technical concepts.

More focused tests are also less brittle, because they are affected by smaller areas of risk. For example, a change in message retry policies will only affect a single technical test, instead of breaking the flow for all business scenarios. Adding a business rule example will not require changes to automation that already handles workflows for similar cases.

When the aspects are mixed, automation code is often too generic and requires a lot of copying and pasting. By splitting business and technical checks, teams get the opportunity to consolidate automation code. Business tests often need to check several success and failure scenarios, technical execution of all those examples is the same. For example, booking a trade, processing it through the approval workflow and lastly checking the end status of the trade. When business tests are clearly separated, it's easy to remove duplication and make such flows easier to maintain and extend.

How to make it work

A mix of business and technical tests is often driven by the misguided opinion that teams should use a single tool for all their tests. Driving the format of a test based on a tool is wrong – it should be exactly the opposite. Tools should be chosen depending on what we want to achieve. For teams stuck in organisations that use a single tool for testing, it's a good trick to rename business-oriented tests as something else (for example, call them executable specifications).

Another good option is to start a discussion around agile testing quadrants and several revisions of that model, all of which are described in *More Agile Testing: Learning Journeys for the Whole Team* by Lisa Crispin and Janet Gregory. Such models visually separate business and technical tests and prompt a discussion on different ways of capturing and executing such tests.

For each test, ask who needs to resolve a potential failure in the future. A failing test might signal a bug (test is right, implementation is wrong), or it might be an unforeseen impact (implementation is right, test is no longer right). If all the people who need to be make the decision work with programming language tools, the test goes in the technical group. If it would not be a technical but a business domain decision, it goes into the business group.

If some potential test failures would be decided by programmers, and some would require business decisions, then a test should be split. For example, a mismatch in XML field ordering coming from a third party doesn't really require a business domain expert to resolve. Neither do asynchronous replies coming out of order, or a database disconnect during an operation. On the other hand, flagging transactions as risky although they are below the currently specified risk threshold might be a bug, or it might be a result of some other change somewhere else in the system, intended to reduce risk exposure. Resolving this question needs someone from the business side.

DON'T AUTOMATE MANUAL TESTS

A common pattern for teams that start with test automation, or development groups that start breaking down silos between testers and developers, is to take existing manual tests and automate them. Unless it's a training exercise for an automation tool, this is almost always a bad idea.

A manual test, even when it's a detailed script, gives testers the opportunity to spot tangential information, such as unexpected events and layout problems. Manual tests provide most value when they are not executed by blindly following just what's written on a piece of paper, but by using the test more as a guideline for investigation. With automated tests, this is not possible, so all that extra value is lost.

Manual tests work well when they provide the context, even if they leave out specifics. For example, a suggestion that a very large file gets processed might inspire people to try out different sizes depending on the most recent software changes and the risks they are investigating. Specifying a file size of exactly 142 megabytes might be over-constraining – it might prove too little in some situations and be complete overkill when investigating something else. On the other hand, automated tests work well only when they are very specific. A machine needs to know exactly how large the input file needs to be, otherwise the test won't be deterministic and repeatable, and potential failure investigation would be too difficult.

Manual tests suffer from the problem of capacity, but they can survive small ambiguities. Compared to a machine, a person can do very little in the same amount of time. This is why manual tests tend to optimise human time – one test prepares the context for another, data is reused to save on set-up time, and

small interdependencies and inconsistencies can be left for a human to resolve. Automated tests don't suffer from the capacity problem as much, so they can easily set the same thing up thousands of times. But they have a different critical constraint. Since automated tests are designed for unattended execution, it's critically important that failures can be investigated quickly. When people automate manual tests, they inherit all the problems with shared context and interdependent impacts. Unfortunately, small inconsistencies can't be resolved by a machine that easily, so such tests tend to be very brittle and require a lot of time for investigating false alerts.

Automating manual tests, without redesigning them first, loses the key benefits of such tests. It also creates a mess in automation that is difficult to investigate and maintain. In a sense, it gives teams the worst of both worlds.

When teams decide to automate a set of existing tests that were previously designed as manual tests, the best way forward is to rewrite and redesign the tests from scratch. Keep the purpose, but throw away pretty much everything else.

Key benefits

Rewriting tests from scratch allows teams to design them properly for unattended execution: decouple tests, remove shared content, improve repeatability and reproducibility, and introduce specifics to help with later investigation.

Because the issue with difficult set-up no longer applies, teams can extend the automated tests to cover many more cases, and increase risk coverage. Redesigning tests allows teams to improve parameterisation, so that new examples can be added quickly.

In addition, manual tests often execute through a user interface, because that's easiest to control. Automation offers the opportunity to skip subsystems or components that aren't critical for a particular scenario, automate at service levels, replace asynchronous waiting with synchronous processing and make tests faster in many other ways. None of these benefits can be achieved if the test script stays the same.

How to make it work

The first step when moving away from a completely manual testing process is to identify the purpose and the risks covered by individual tests. To save time in execution, it's common for a single manual test to check lots of different things or to address several risks. For automated tests, it's much better to address each of those aspects with separate tests, or even entire test suites. I generally try to break a single process into individual rules, describe workflows separately from decision points, remove generalisations and revisit necessary inputs, outputs and boundaries for each test separately.

The next step is to split out test aspects that require human insight from those that can be measured by machine. There is a lot of value in a human observing how something works, investigating along tangential paths and exploring unknown or unexpected impacts. Automated tests should only check for deterministic, pre-defined outcomes, freeing up people to explore non-deterministic outputs and identify unexpected outcomes. Don't even try to automate those aspects of tests, because you'll just be wasting time and losing all the value.

Get developers and testers to rewrite tests together, because they can have a discussion on the best way to cover particular risks and what additional cases need to be considered. When teams rewrite business-oriented tests, make sure that they are reviewed by stakeholders and domain experts.

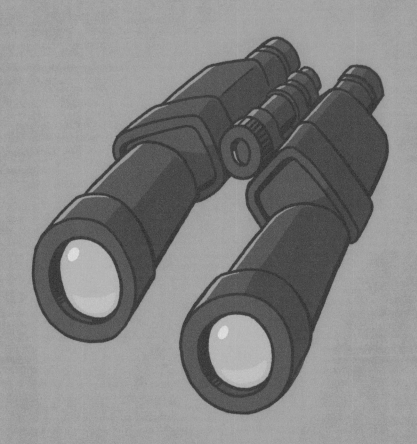

IMPROVING TESTABILITY

WRAP SYNCHRONOUS DATABASE TESTS IN TRANSACTIONS

Tests involving a database require teams to make careful compromises between isolation, reliability and speed of feedback.

One option is for tests to talk to a production-like data source. This makes them very reliable, because the environment in which they run is similar to the that of the target platform. But setting up production-like databases is not practical for anything apart from the most trivial reference data sources. Production databases tend to be big, messy, full of real-world data, and just copying the data files for use by a set of tests is often several orders of magnitude longer than the tests themselves would take to run. A common approach is to have a single data source for all the tests, which speeds up feedback slightly, but requires teams to sacrifice isolation. One test can mess things up easily for other tests, and generally any idea of parallel test execution goes out of the window.

A common alternative is for tests to execute using a simplified, minimised data set, which is faster to set up.

This speeds up feedback but sacrifices reliability. Data-driven systems often experience issues when they hit unexpected real-world information, and tests running on an idealised, simple data set rarely encounter such problems. And even with smaller data sets, starting up a database process instance might take several minutes, making it impractical to shut down and restart for every test.

The third solution, common with teams that develop most of their software using object-oriented platforms, is to run tests against a specialised testing database. Ideally, object-oriented data access libraries should take care of database access, so the same test can in theory be executed against any type of data source. This leads to tests with in-memory databases which require no disk access and can be started inside the test runner process. Feedback is much faster, tests are completely isolated, but unfortunately this approach makes tests highly unreliable. For example, one team we worked with executed most of their tests using HSQLDB, an in-memory Java database. Their production system was running on Oracle. All tests could happily pass, only for the system to fail in production because of vendor-specific SQL syntax. Such tests are worse than no automation, because they are highly misleading.

In cases where the activity under test is synchronous, and involves only one operating system process (so it's not distributed), there is a much simpler solution. Just wrap tests in database transactions, and roll back transactions at the end of each test.

Key benefits

Most database management systems automatically isolate transactions, so tests running in different transactions are fully isolated. This allows teams to execute tests in parallel, speeding up feedback.

Rolling back transactions after each test ensures that subsequent tests don't see any unwanted changes in reference data, which helps to avoid false alarms. For example, one of our clients had to allocate trades against a particular fund, and to make tests repeatable each test would use a different fund. They only had a few thousand funds set up in the database, so at some point every week the tests would start failing because there were no more clean funds available. Wrapping tests in transactions and rolling the changes back allowed the team to keep running the tests indefinitely. Although trades would be allocated during a test, the allocations would magically disappear before the next test started.

This approach also significantly simplifies clean-up procedures after testing. Without a roll-back, each test has to explicitly remove the information it created, which increases the amount of automation code, makes tests more expensive and more difficult to maintain, and makes tests longer. Rolling back database transactions is often instantaneous and requires no special software code to be written and maintained.

In addition, this makes data-driven tests instantly repeatable. With custom clean-up procedures, teams often spend a lot of time ensuring that a test can run repeatedly. A classic example is a test that tries to register a new user with a particular username. Unless the database is correctly cleaned up, duplicate username checks might prevent the same test from running repeatedly. If the test runs inside a database transaction, when the transaction rolls back, the newly created user will disappear.

How to make it work

Transaction control should be done globally, because one test outside control can mess things up for thousands of transactional tests. Even worse, problems like this are difficult to troubleshoot, because the offending test will likely pass, but randomly break tests that follow it.

The best way to set transaction control is to do it globally, in the testing framework rather than in each individual test. For example, when working with FitNesse for a financial service client, we implemented a thin wrapper around the standard test runner that would start a transaction, delegate to the normal runner, and just roll back the transaction at the end. This made all tests instantly isolated and reversible, without the need for individuals to remember to add this configuration to each test.

If your testing tool does not allow global wrappers, think about adding transaction management code to test suite set-ups and tear-downs.

SET UP BEFORE ASYNCHRONOUS DATA TESTS, DON'T CLEAN UP AFTER

When a data-driven process has several asynchronous components, using database transactions to isolate tests just isn't practical. If the system is distributed as well, resetting the data might require time that your team just doesn't have. Sometimes the team can't clean up the data because it's not even under their control. For all those reasons, full isolation with clean external data sources before each test is often impractical with asynchronous components.

To get round this problem, teams often run tests in partial isolation, and have each test cleaning up after itself. Although this might sound good in theory, in practice it creates a lot of problems. Clean-up procedures are mostly written from the perspective of tests that pass, and often don't work when a test fails. Similarly, when a bug causes one test to fail, many testing tools won't execute the rest of the test, so clean-up code is often skipped. Tests also might be interrupted for many reasons, including something external or users stopping a long-running test batch that got stuck.

An invalid starting state can create false alarms, causing teams to waste time investigating non-existent failures. With large suites, this problem is even worse, because failures can cascade and spread easily. One test might break due to an invalid starting state, and then leave the external data in an inconsistent state for many other tests. This makes pinpointing the cause of the problem even more difficult. Data-driven state problems are temporal, environment-dependent, difficult to troubleshoot and reproduce, so even with a lot of work, it's impossible to be sure that they have been completely fixed.

It may sound logical that each test should clean up after itself, but it's far more practical to clean up environments in test set-ups, before each test executes. Whenever possible, rely on set-up code to sort out an inconsistent data state. Feel free to include clean-up procedures after testing but don't rely on them being always executed.

Key benefits

Ensuring environment and data consistency in test set-up code is a bit trickier to get right than performing clean-ups, because a test won't know what was executed before it. So set-ups need to be much more defensive and check for more things. But the effort pays off quickly.

First of all, tests will be better isolated. Problems in one test won't cascade to many other tests. When a bug causes a test failure, you will only need to investigate that single test, not 500 other false alarms, saving valuable time.

In addition, if there is no post-test clean-up code, you can inspect failures more easily. When a bug causes a test to fail, clean-up code might remove important evidence, and that's exactly when we need detailed information on what went wrong. If most of the data manipulation is in the set-up code, a failing test leaves all the mess it created for people to investigate quickly and easily.

Relying more on preparation than clean-up also allows teams to optimise slow tasks. For example, set-up code can quickly check if the database state is good enough for a particular test and avoid running unnecessary preparations if it is.

How to make it work

Ideally, each test should be able to set up the external environment for itself, but sometimes this isn't possible. In such cases, the set-up code should at least check if the external state is consistent enough for the test to execute. If it is not, issue an alert about the invalid starting position without allowing the test to run. It's much better to see an invalid state warning than a false failure.

When working with external resources, especially time-consuming tasks, try to introduce some kind of version check that can short-circuit the set-up stage if it is not needed. One team we worked with introduced triggers for all reference data tables, that automatically updated a version number in the test data control table. This allowed tests to execute truncation only if the reference data had been modified. If none of the previous tests had changed the reference data, subsequent tests could just run without preparing the database. If a single version number won't do the trick for you, think about using checksums on important blocks of data.

Another possibility is to perform data set-up for entire groups of tests (or test suites), and ensure that individual tests in that group work with different objects. This allows one long-running set-up to execute once for the entire group.

Avoid removing evidence of failures in test clean-ups, and never depend on clean-ups actually completing if you can't explicitly control them. Use clean-up procedures after tests just for optimistic resource de-allocation, for example, freeing up database connections and unsubscribing from external queues.

INTRODUCE BUSINESS TIME

Time-based features tend to be very difficult to test properly. A typical example is post-processing that needs to happen at the end of a time-based event, such as re-enabling buttons on a form after a 300 millisecond (ms) animation. Many teams write a test that pauses for 300 ms, then checks the button state. This approach is problematic from two perspectives: it's not really deterministic, and it's delaying feedback. Although specifying the exact number of milliseconds sounds deterministic, it's actually difficult to guarantee millisecond accuracy for asynchronous processes on most operating systems, because they are just not built for real-time processing. A memory clean-up job, disk access or something similar might take over and delay the animation just long enough for the test to fail occasionally. A potential workaround is to specify a longer period – say a second or so, but then we're not really testing that the buttons are re-enabled when they need to be. Adding any kind of artificial delay to

automated tests is always bad, because it prolongs test execution and delays feedback. Defensive tests that wait longer than really needed, to avoid small timing differences, don't help either. Although a second might not sound too much, multiply that by a few hundred test cases and a few dozen runs of such cases every day, and things start to look quite serious.

The problems get even worse with longer time periods. Imagine that you want to prove that an overnight job will aggregate all credit card transactions from the previous day into a report, or that a discount offer will expire in thirty days. Nobody will wait a month to get the results of an automated test, so such tests are typically automated using magic time constants. For example, discount offers are specified using ONE_MONTH_AGO, and automation code replaces that value with a concrete date. The problem with this approach is that it can hide quite a few important assumptions about the meaning of rules. For example, what date is ONE_MONTH_AGO on 30th of March? Time differences sound simple, but leap years, daylight saving and time zones can easily turn them into a mess.

A pretty good solution for time-based constraints is to design the system to use a concept of business time instead of relying on the operating system clock. For testing purposes, the business time can then be manipulated easily. For production use, the business time can follow the operating system clock.

Key benefits

Decoupling business time from operating system time makes tests much more reliable. We can move the business clock 299 milliseconds into the future and check that buttons are disabled, then move it one more millisecond and check that they are enabled. All this can happen instantaneously, without causing any feedback delay or blocking the testing system.

Introducing business time allows teams to be much more precise in describing their tests, which helps to discover wrong assumptions and open up a good discussion on actual requirements.

An analytics company we worked with used magic constants for time values in their tests. When we started re-writing tests using business time and concrete values, the team discovered a huge misunderstanding between developers and business stakeholders. Their system generated reports for pre-defined time periods such as 'yesterday' and 'last month'. The developers considered yesterday to be the previous calendar day in the time zone where the servers were based. For business stakeholders, 'yesterday' meant the previous calendar day for whatever time zone the user was in.

Business time, since it doesn't necessarily follow the operating system clock, also makes things easier to control in production if needed. For example, if a bug is discovered in monthly reports, it's easy to rerun the reporting engine for previous periods and get data as on a particular day.

How to make it work

A typical way of implementing business time is to separate out an application clock component, and make all other components use it instead of the operating system clock. Then it's easy to roll time forwards and backwards. This approach requires that the whole application stack is under the control of the delivery team.

When the application involves external components that can't be easily modified, such as database procedures that automatically time-stamp records, a potential workaround is to set the system clock on the test environment. This is a good strategy if two conditions are met: the entire application stack can run on a single machine (so the clock can easily be moved for everything at once) and third-party components won't explode if the time starts flowing backwards. If you use this option, it's often good to put the application stack and test runners on different machines, so that the tests remotely control the application. This avoids false test duration reports, and provides a source of real-world time that the application clock can return to after testing.

If you're working with third-party components that only expect the time to flow in one direction, and randomly fail if you start playing with the system clock, consider re-architecting the areas under your control so that you can test them in isolation.

PROVIDE ATOMIC EXTERNAL RESOURCES

Resources created asynchronously, or outside the main testing process, are one of the major causes of instability for automated tests. A good example of this is a trade reconciliation system at an investment fund we worked with. Most of their tests requested a daily export of trades from different sources and cross-checked the trades. One of the sources would export a file and send it using FTP. The tests would first request the file export, then wait for a file to appear, and finally load trades and compare them against internal records. The problem was that many of the tests would randomly fail, but on subsequent runs they would pass, while some other tests that had worked would fail. Their test execution system would run all the tests five times and mark the tests that passed at least once as OK. This is a very problematic strategy. The number five was chosen because it seemed to make most problems go away, but sometimes even the tests that had five failures were actually OK when executed separately. On the other hand, this created huge feedback delays. Tests that rely on remote FTP are slow anyway, but running them five times just made things ridiculously slow, without guaranteeing accuracy.

We traced the problem down to the trade loader occasionally missing a few trades from the remote file. The tests were checking only if the file existed, not if the remote process had finished transferring all the data. Because the test trades were relatively small and few, the initial file creation would be quick enough in most cases for this to work. But sometimes, due to network delays or slightly larger files, a test would see the file before all the contents had been transferred. The test process would then start loading the trades while the remote transfer was still copying the file over, and omit the remaining trades.

Failures such as this one are tricky to identify and troubleshoot, because they depend on small differences in the environment. Such problems do not appear on a developer test system because everything runs on a fast local network, while they can start randomly popping up on a more integrated production-like environment. This often leads to bugs falsely classified as not reproducible, and the infamous 'it works on my machine' effect.

Whenever a test needs to access external resources, in particular if they are created asynchronously or transferred across networks, ensure that the resources are hidden until they are fully complete. Make them atomic – the appearance of the resource should also mean that it is ready for use.

Key benefits

Atomic external resources prevent false alarms and save a lot of time by making test execution more reliable. After we had changed the file handling for the trade reconciliation tests, they needed to run only once, instead of five times. The team also spent considerably less time diagnosing errors.

Another benefit of this technique is that it makes resource handling easier in production systems. If tests can get incomplete data, it's likely that the underlying process in the system under test can experience the same problem. By designing atomic resource handling for tests, it becomes easier to provide such resources to production systems as well, and avoid occasional nasty bugs that are very difficult to troubleshoot.

How to make it work

If possible, design the system so that it creates an external resource file under a temporary name, and when it completes and closes the file, renames it in accordance with the final expected output. Writing file content is normally a buffered operation, so files may appear even though they are incomplete. Renaming, on the other hand, is normally an atomic operation. For multi-process exports where file names are important and you can't just create a temporary name, use different folders for file creation and file consumption. Moving files across folders is similar to renaming, typically atomic on today's operating systems.

These two approaches require modifying the external resource file creation process. If this is not possible, but there is a separate file transfer process, consider using a different mechanism to indicate that the transfer is complete. For example, send a message to a queue or create an empty marker file with the same name and a different extension when the resource file transfer is complete. The loader process can then look for the marker file instead of the resource file. Because the marker file content is ignored, the problem of loading partial data is resolved.

If you cannot change either the file creation or the transfer process, consider having the tests open files for exclusive writing instead of reading. Most operating systems do not lock files for reading, but have an option to lock files for writing. By requesting an exclusive write lock, the process that consumes a file can be blocked until the transfer completes. The downside of this approach is that the file reader has to run under wider system privileges in testing than in production, which might hide some other problems.

The fourth option is to check for file existence, wait for a short period of time, and then check if the file is growing or not. This is obviously not ideal, because network latency and file system buffering can cause a file to appear as stable while the data is still coming in. Use this technique as a last resort, if the other approaches are not feasible.

WAIT FOR EVENTS, NOT TIME

Most modern software is built to run across several machines. Mobile devices and web interfaces often depend on remote data, service-oriented architectures split processes into multiple components and cloud-based applications synchronise local information with popular storage services. All these processes require testing, and by design they are often asynchronous. This means that tests involving such components involve waiting on a remote resource to retrieve or upload data or to complete some long-running operation. The most popular way of handle this testing is to include time-based waiting, such as steps that require a test to wait three seconds.

Time-based waiting is the equivalent of going out on the street and waiting for half an hour in the rain upon receiving a thirty-minute delivery estimate for pizza, only to discover that the pizza guy came along a different road and dropped it off 10 minutes ago. If you wait for a set period of time, both you and the pizza will be cold. It's far better to wait in for the delivery.

The big problem with time-based waiting is that it is highly environment-dependent. In typical developer environments, where multiple services run on the same machine, the required wait time is much lower than on a realistic production-like environment. This causes tests to pass on developer machines but fail during integration testing, or requires developers to slow down their tests unnecessarily.

Additionally, temporary network latency or other processes running on the same machines can slow down remote operations. This presents a major problem when it comes to choosing the right length of time to wait. Set it too low, and tests will flicker and report false alarms. Set it too high, and you slow down feedback significantly even when the network is not busy.

Even if adding a few seconds to a single test doesn't create a problem, this practice just does not scale. With a few hundred tests, the additional feedback delay can easily extend to hours. Overly long wait cycles cause developers to skip running such tests frequently, so issues propagate to integration environments and get discovered too late.

Coupled with slow feedback cycles from test suites, this often causes huge coordination problems for organisations with multiple teams. When one team breaks the integration test environment, the other teams don't get fast feedback about newly introduced problems and cross-team issues easily accumulate.

Whenever possible, avoid waiting for a period of time, but instead wait for an event to happen. For example, wait for a message to appear on a queue, or for a file to appear on a file system. Tests can then be automated to wait until that event happens.

Key benefits

Waiting for events instead of time is critical because it speeds up feedback. Any arbitrary time limit will be either too short or too long, and cause tests to flicker or delay feedback unnecessarily. When a test is waiting on an event, it can proceed immediately after that event instead of delaying feedback further. On large test suites this trick can easily save hours of execution time. This means that developers are more likely to execute such tests locally. In organisations with multiple teams, this means that problems created by one team are likely to be caught before their code is integrated with the work of other teams, significantly reducing interruptions.

Waiting on events instead of time also makes tests less environment-specific. Slow networks and busy machines are no longer a problem, because the criterion for proceeding takes those factors into consideration. This means fewer false alarms, so the teams spend less time investigating fake issues.

How to make it work

Asynchronous operation tools and libraries often support completion notifications. These are a great alternative to waiting for time. For example, background data retrieval in web browsers can notify the application after the transfer completes. In most cases, the system under test already uses such notifications to avoid working with incomplete information, and it's easy to just expose or extend such notification to a test system.

If the remote communication processes are not under your control and you can't expose the notifications easily, then consider changing the remote process to generate an additional event. For example, push a message to a queue when the database write ends. The test can then listen to the queue before proceeding.

If the remote process is not under your control, check if it generates any log files or additional outputs. If so, it's often a good idea to process those outputs and generate an event based on them, for example, send a list of all completed operation identifiers to a queue.

If it's not possible to create a blocking operation, it might be possible to periodically check for an existence of a resource. For example, instead of waiting for five seconds for a web page to reload, check if the page contains a particular title or element every 100 milliseconds. For remote data-driven processes, check if a transaction record is in the database. Periodic checking (also called sampling) works well when tests expect something to happen, but they aren't really good in describing that something shouldn't happen, for example, that user details fail to be registered. In that case, it's often better to describe an alternative event. See the section *Ask 'what happens instead?'* for more information on this technique.

SPLIT DATA GENERATORS FROM TESTS

Tests for groups of operations often do not really depend on attributes of individual actions. A typical example is loading 100,000 trades to see if the system can take them in quickly enough. The details of individual trades might be required to actually automate the process, but they are not really relevant for the purpose of that particular test. Specifying each of the trade transactions in detail would make the test impossible to understand, but naively using 100,000 copies of one transaction might not be an adequate check. In cases like this, it's far better to build a generator for the test data, for example one that creates trades by randomly assigning funds or accounts, and let the test just specify how many trades it needs.

Systems that require automatically generated data for tests can often use the same inputs for many different test scenarios, with slight modifications. But data generators are often so tightly integrated into tests that they cannot be easily tweaked. Many teams end up duplicating similar generators all over their test suite.

If you have to run a lot of tests driven by generated data, one of the best tricks to improve feedback and reduce maintenance costs is to completely decouple data generators from individual test scenarios. Write them as separate libraries, or even separate processes.

Key benefits

Splitting test data set-up from test execution instantly provides a lot more flexibility for both. Each component can be maintained separately, and generators can be replaced by better versions without any changes to tests.

If a test uses randomly generated data and fails, there is always a possibility that the data was invalid. When the data generator is split from the test, it's much easier to run it separately and validate the data if needed.

When the underlying infrastructure makes test automation or maintenance difficult, dividing data

IMPROVING TESTABILITY

generators and tests makes it possible to reuse tests. Teams can plug different data generators into a single automated test, simplifying test maintenance significantly. For example, a team can use the same test with European and American trades just by swapping the data file.

Different generators can also help teams to trade off speed of feedback against risk coverage. For example, a team can use randomly generated trades on the internal testing environment, but use a slower process to replay last month's trades from the production database for user acceptance testing. This trick can also be used to reduce reliance on specialist hardware. For example, a team can use pseudo-random numbers during development, but run the same tests using a hardware random number generator before deployment to production.

By separating data generators from tests, teams also get an option to reuse generated data. Several teams we worked with reduced the total execution time of their test suites by an order of magnitude by grouping related tests together and generating the data only once, in the test suite set-up.

How to make it work

If possible, save test data into files and use a simple data format. Avoid binary information if you can, and instead use human-readable text. Avoid position-based columns or complex nested structures, and use separators such as spaces or commas that humans can understand. Position-based data saves a bit of programming time, but you'll lose the possibility of manually validating the data. If the generated data is human-readable, you can easily give it to a domain expert to sense-check in case of failure. When the data format is human-readable, people can also easily modify and hand-craft inputs. Text files can also be placed in version control systems easily, if you need to have an audit trail of changes.

If the generators are complex or time-consuming to run, enable tests to reuse them by connecting the generator parameters with the resulting file. For generators with only a few arguments, a good solution is to indicate the contents of a file in its name. For example, trades-10000-US.txt for the generated trades file that uses US and 10000 as parameters. For more complex configurations, a good trick is to use a separate configuration file, and name the output file by just changing the extension. For example, the generator would read trades-166.cfg, and create trades-166.txt.

This allows individual tests to check if the relevant file already exists and avoid running generators repeatedly. It also allows the team to regenerate the data using the same arguments if they fix bugs in the generators or use a completely different generator.

Decoupling generators from test execution does, however, introduce the problem of trust. If you're planning to use multiple generators for the same tests, or if you expect people to manually modify and craft input data, it might be a good idea to run some basic data validity checks on the data before a test. Such quick sanity checks can save a lot of time later, because you will not have to investigate false alarms caused by invalid data.

MINIMISE UI INTERACTIONS

The user interface (UI) is, quite naturally, the first thing that comes to the mind of everyday users when they think about a software system. That's why most acceptance criteria provided by users talk about user interface interactions. There is nothing wrong with starting a discussion about testing with such examples, but beware of accepting them as the be-all and end-of all testing.

UI interactions in tests often describe how something can be tested, not the actual purpose of the test (see the section *Describe 'what', not 'how'* for information on why that's problematic). UI automation often makes tests unnecessarily slow, environment-dependent and fragile, severely limiting the effectiveness of tests.

Because a test executed through a UI typically brings the entire application stack together, it is constrained by consistency and validity rules applicable to the entire system, which can get in the way of exhaustive testing. For example, email systems often prevent users from sending too many messages in a short period of time. Turning on that constraint might be great to test sending limits, but it makes it almost impossible to prepare the context for testing how the system works when users have thousands of messages in their inbox. When the entire application stack comes together, such constraints cannot be easily disabled.

On the other hand, the UI cannot be tested well just by deterministic checks. The many unexpected things that can happen with a user interface mostly require a human eye to spot and a critical human brain to analyse. Even if all features work as expected, the UI might be unusable due to poor alignment of visual controls, colour contrast, visual and spatial organisation of elements and general look and feel. That's why it's far better to get a human to look over the critical

aspects of a UI, instead of letting a machine decide that it all works as expected.

Unless a test is actually derisking something crucial within a UI, try to rephrase UI-related examples so that they talk about business domain concepts. Keep UI actions only in tests that deal with UI-specific risks.

Key benefits

Minimising UI interactions makes tests faster and more reliable. The UI is often the slowest and the most brittle part of a system, and small changes in it break tests easily. For example, converting a button into a link will break all tests that depend on the button, even if they are checking something completely different and using the button just to set up test data. By avoiding the UI layer where it is not actually relevant for the purpose of the test, teams can save a lot of troubleshooting time and speed up feedback, while still keeping the same level of risk coverage.

By avoiding UI interactions, we can also work around full-stack validation and consistency, specifying and automating examples that validate individual features around their particular boundaries. For example, we can pump thousands of messages into a database directly and validate inbox performance with large lists, rather than trying to work round throttling constraints in the upper layers of the application stack.

How to make it work

Even when tests need to execute through the UI, minimise the part of the test that actually simulates user actions. Evaluate which parts of the tests are actually dealing with UI-specific risks, and try to automate everything else by avoiding the UI. Set-up and clean-up tasks serve to make tests reliable and repeatable, but they do not actually deal with the user interface risk (or, more precisely, they should not – if a set-up task is testing things, it should be broken into several tests). Such auxiliary tasks are good candidates to pull out and automate differently. For example, we worked with a client whose tests all started by launching an administrative application, registering a user, approving the account, registering a payment card, approving the payment card and transferring money into the account, all simply to create a valid clean customer account for the rest of the test. This took about ninety seconds for each test. The delivery team replaced all of it with a single step called 'Given a valid customer account with 100 USD', which executed directly using

a database. From a minute and a half per test, they were creating valid accounts in in milliseconds without increasing any the risk. If anything, they made the tests more reliable.

If it's not possible to directly manipulate the context of a test, it's often possible to execute the appropriate set-up or clean-up commands just below the skin of the application. For example, instead of launching a browser and waiting for asynchronous javascript events, simulate HTTP calls that the application would make to the back end. This will still be an order of magnitude faster and more reliable than full UI execution, and removes what is typically the weakest link from the application stack.

If the application does not provide a sensible way of directly automating the context below the UI, it's often worth introducing a test-specific network interface to load the application context.

For example, for testing a mobile application, different tests might require different internal memory state, internal file contents, and application state to run. Changing the context correctly from one test to another will probably require slow and error-prone manual intervention through the user interface. If we're testing the application by running it in a mobile phone simulator, we can reload the entire simulator each time and set up the context that way, but this would probably be prohibitively slow to run hundreds of tests. Alternatively, we can set up a TCP channel or a web service in the mobile application to control the test context remotely. The test framework can use the control service to reliably and quickly prepare the stage for each test, under the skin of the application. Such remote controls for testing should, of course, be packaged only with test versions of the application.

SEPARATE DECISIONS, WORKFLOWS AND TECHNICAL INTERACTIONS

Any good test automation book will suggest that user interface interactions need to be minimised or completely avoided. However, there are legitimate cases where the user interface is the only thing that can actually execute a relevant test. A common example is where the architecture dictates that most of the business logic sits in the user interface layer (such applications are often called 'legacy' even by people who write them, but they are still being written). Another common situation is when an opaque, third-party component drives an important business process, but has no sensible automation hooks built into it. In such cases, teams often resort to record-and-replay tools with horrible unmaintainable scripts. They create tests that are so difficult to control and so expensive to maintain that it's only possible to afford to check a very small subset of interesting scenarios. Teams in such situations often completely give up on any kind of automation after a while.

There are two key problems with such tests. One is that they are slow, as they often require a full application stack to execute. The other is that they are extremely brittle. Small user interface changes, such as moving a button on the screen somewhere else, or changing it to a hyperlink, break all the tests that use that element. Changes in the application workflow, such as requiring people to be logged in to see some previously public information, or introducing a back-end authorisation requirement for an action, pretty much break all the tests instantly.

There might not be anything we can do to make such tests run as fast as the ones below the user interface, but there are definitely some nice tricks that can significantly reduce the cost of maintenance of such

tests, enough to make large test suites manageable. One of the most important ideas is to apply a three-layer approach to automation: divide business-oriented decisions, workflows and technical interactions into separate layers. Then ensure that all business decision tests reuse the same workflow components, and ensure that workflow components share technical interactions related to common user interface elements.

We've used this approach with many clients, from financial trading companies working with thick-client administrative applications, to companies developing consumer-facing websites. It might not be a silver bullet for all possible UI automation situations, but it comes pretty close to that, and deserves at least to be the starting point for discussions.

Key benefits

A major benefit of the three-layer approach, compared to record-and-replay tests, is much easier maintenance. Changes are localised. If a button suddenly becomes a hyperlink, all that needs to change is one technical activity. Workflows depending on that button continue to work. If a workflow gets a new step, or loses one, the only thing that needs to change is the workflow component. All technical activities stay untouched, as do any business rule specifications that use the workflow. Finally, because workflows are reused to check business decisions, it's easy to add more business checks.

The three-layer design pattern is inspired by similar ideas from the popular page object pattern, but instead of tying business tests too tightly to current web page structures, it decouples all common types of change. Tests automated using page objects are easily broken by workflow changes that require modifications to transitions between pages or affect the order of interactions. Because of this, the three-layer approach is better for applications with non-trivial workflows. Applications with a lot of messy user interface logic often need a good set of integration tests as well as business checks. Another big benefit of the three-layer approach is that the bottom layer, technical interactions, can be easily reused for technical integration tests. This reduces the overall cost of test maintenance even further, and allows the delivery team to automate new tests more easily.

How to make it work

Most test automation tools work with one or two layers of information. Tools such as FitNesse, Concordion or Cucumber provide two layers: the business specification and the automation code. Developer-oriented tools such as Selenium RC and unit-testing tools tend to offer only one layer, the automation code. So do tester-oriented tools. This misleads many teams into flattening their layer hierarchy too soon. Automation layers for most of these tools are written using standard programming languages, which allow for abstractions and layering. For example, using Concordion, the top-level (human readable specification) can be reserved for the business-decision layer, and the automation code below can be structured to utilise workflow components, which in turn utilise technical activity components.

Some tools, such as Cucumber, allow some basic reuse and abstraction in the test specification (top level) as well. This theoretically makes it possible to use the bottom automation layer only for technical interactions, and push the top two layers into the business-readable part of the stack. Unless your team has a great many more testers than developers, it's best to avoid doing this. In effect, people will end up programming in plain text, without any support from modern development tool capabilities such as automated refactoring, contextual search and compilation checks.

USE PRODUCTION METRICS FOR EXPENSIVE TESTS

Many teams shy away from testing anything that is expensive or difficult to measure. Yet there are entire classes of difficult tests that are incredibly valuable, and although they are expensive, the value far outweighs the cost. For example, it's cheap to test usability improvements by comparing the resulting screens with wire-frame requirements, but the true test for usability improvements is whether users are actually doing something faster or not. Actual changes to user productivity have traditionally been a lot more expensive to measure than compliance with wire-frame diagrams, but at the same time that information is a lot more valuable. In their paper *Online Experimentation at Microsoft*, Kohavi, Crook and others have some sobering statistics: only about one third of all ideas implemented in software actually improve the metrics they were designed to improve. Checking those metrics directly, rather than just measuring compliance with

requirements, can help prune out unsuccessful ideas, reduce software maintenance costs, and deliver more value to users.

Modern software delivery processes and technologies make it easy to significantly shift the costs of such measurements. With frequent iterative releases, the risk introduced by changes goes down significantly. We can then actually start testing overall impacts cheaply and easily by observing the effects of small changes on the production environment. For example, set up production-usage metrics to measure how long it takes for users to complete tasks in real life, then compare the measurements before and after a software change is deployed.

Instead of just accepting that something is difficult to test and ignoring it, investigate whether you can measure it in the production environment. If so, extend your testing strategy to include such measurements. State expectations, as you would normally through examples and specifications, and make sure they are performed. Report on them as you would for other testing activities, even though they are happening after a feature was delivered to users. Don't consider a story done until it has been verified fully that way.

Key benefits

Testing key usage metrics in production can greatly reduce the cost of measurements that were traditionally very expensive. For example, performance testing for mid-sized websites typically requires installing production-like hardware, dealing with expensive storage and complex configurations, and then simulating large groups of users accessing the system concurrently. Such simulations always carry risks that the simulated user activities do not realistically reflect peak-time usage, and that the hardware constraints don't match the real production environment. For example, the test environment might have a bottleneck in disk input/output while production environments tend to have bottlenecks in CPU processing. With sufficiently frequent small changes, the performance risks of individual releases are minimal, so we can look at real usage trends to collect performance metrics. We don't need a separate testing environment, and we won't risk missing some critical aspect of real usage in simulations.

Production metrics are often collected ad hoc, and mostly used only for troubleshooting problems. They are rarely comparable across different versions and longer periods of time. However, when teams actively work with production metrics as part of their testing strategies, they tend to be much more precise about what they measure, why and how the information is collected, and ensure that trends are comparable over time. This leads to an interesting side effect of conducting tests in production: teams get interesting documentation for future impact analysis.

How to make it work

Production usage measurements are primarily useful for cross-cutting concerns, such as service level agreements for performance or usability improvements. This might be an effective approach to testing quality aspects related to the usefulness or success of a product (the top two levels of Maslow-style pyramids as described in the section *Define a shared big-picture view of quality*).

If software is not designed for collecting metrics upfront, it might be prohibitively expensive to measure such things. Once you've identified the measurements that might be useful to take in production, discuss with the team whether the software needs to be changed to allow easier collection of them. When you can influence the design of software, knowing what activities you want to measure, it becomes very cheap to run the tests.

For web-based tools, online analytic systems such as Google Analytics make actual user activities easy to report on, as long as the team knows what to look for. For non-web applications, custom monitoring metrics can be easily built in and collected through log files or periodic network access.

MANAGING LARGE TEST SUITES

MAKE DEVELOPERS RESPONSIBLE FOR CHECKING

Many organisations start with test automation as an auxiliary activity – it needs to be done, but without interrupting the development schedule. This often leads to test automation specialists working after development, or even entire teams of people charged with making testing faster and cheaper. This is a false premise, and can lead to a lot of trouble later on.

By decoupling development and test automation, teams either introduce a lot of duplicated work or unnecessarily delay feedback. Manually running all the tests during development is rarely sustainable, so such teams allow development to officially finish without any serious testing. If a developer receives feedback about potential problems only after a different team automates tests, the code that needs to be fixed might have been changed by some other people meanwhile. This introduces a further delay, because developers need to coordinate more and research other potential changes to fix problems.

In addition, when specialists are hired to automate tests, they are often overwhelmed by work. Ten developers can produce a lot more code than a single person can test, so specialist automation often introduces a bottleneck. The delivery pipeline slows down to the speed of test automation, or software gets shipped without completed testing. The first scenario is horrible because the organisation loses the ability to ship software quickly. The second scenario is horrible because developers stop caring about testing, and automated tests then just come to seem like a waste of time and money. Developers do not design the system to be testable, and it becomes even more difficult to automate tests, causing more delay between development and testing. It's a lose-lose situation.

Separate automation specialists rarely have the insight into system internals, so the only option for them is to automate tests end-to-end. Such tests will be unnecessarily slow and brittle, and take a lot of time to maintain. Slow, difficult tests bolster the argument for not disrupting the critical delivery path with tests.

Test automation specialists often use tools that developers are not familiar with, so it is not easy for them to ask for help from the rest of the team. Any potential test automation problems have to be investigated by test automation experts, which creates a further bottleneck. It's a vicious circle where testing only gets further separated from delivery, creating more problems and even slower feedback.

The only economically sustainable way of writing and automating hundreds of tests is to make developers responsible for doing it. Avoid using specialist groups and test automation experts. Give people who implement functionality the responsibility to execute tests, and ensure they have the necessary information to do it properly.

Key benefits

When the same people are tasked with changing code and automating the related tests, tests are automated a lot more reliably and execute much faster. Programmers have insight into system internals, they can use lots of different automation hooks, and they can design and automate tests depending on the real area of risk, not just on an end-to-end basis. This also means that developers can use the tools they like and are familiar with, so any potential problem investigations can be delegated to a larger group of people and not just automation tool specialists.

In addition, when developers are responsible for automation, they will design the system to make it easy to control and observe functionality in the first place. They will build modules that can be tested in isolation, and decouple them so tests can run quickly. This brings the benefit of faster testing, but a modular design also makes it easier to evolve the system and implement future requests for change.

When developers are responsible for test automation, the tests will deliver fast feedback. The time between introducing a problem and spotting it is significantly shorter, and the risk of someone else modifying the underlying code meanwhile is eliminated.

These three factors significantly change the economics of test automation. Tests run faster, cheaper, they are more reliable, and the system is more modular so it's easier to write tests. There is no artificial bottleneck later in testing, and no need to choose between higher quality and faster deployment.

How to make it work

A common argument against letting developers automate tests is to ensure independent feedback and avoid tunnel vision. The right way to counter this is to ensure that the right people are involved in designing the tests. Developers should be responsible for automating the tests, but the entire team (including business stakeholders and testers) should be involved in deciding what needs to be tested.

Teams without test automation experience should not hire automation experts to take on the work. External experts should only be hired to teach developers how to use a particular tool for automation, and provide advice on how best to design tests.

Teams with a high risk of automation being done wrongly can further reduce the risk by pairing up testers and developers during automation work, and by running some quick exploratory tests to investigate the automation code.

DESIGN TESTS TOGETHER WITH OTHER TEAMS

94

In large organisations, the biggest risks to quality often come from cross-team boundaries. This is particularly problematic for fast-moving iterative delivery, where teams make design choices and modify interfaces more frequently than they can update documentation. If the work of one team depends on the work of another, the first team's work can get blocked in delivery, waiting for information or for an updated version of a component. Situations like this require dependent teams to constantly adjust to unexpected changes from upstream teams. This leads to a lot of unnecessary rework, both in development and testing.

Modern architectural solutions such as microservices reduce this problem by requiring other teams to only use well-known published APIs. However, even these solutions require some level of cross-team communication. Also, such solutions aren't universally applicable. Many legacy systems, especially in larger organisations, just aren't built for that kind of division of responsibility. In addition, treating all other teams in the same organisation as completely third-party external users is probably an overkill.

A potential solution, which we've seen work well in many contexts, is for client team and upstream team members to work together on designing tests for cross-team boundaries. This can take the form of a shared set of tests for an API, or just a common agreement on key scenarios and risks to explore with shared data. It's critical to involve both the people delivering a module and people using that module to define tests together. Ideally, the tests should be co-owned by the teams, so that people remember to communicate changes.

For example, an analytics organisation we worked with had several teams working on their data warehouse solution. Three teams worked on importing source data from various third parties. Two teams dealt with cleaning up internal records, and organising the data in a way that made it easy to pull out reports. Three client-oriented teams produced reports for different lines of business. The client report teams were often blocked by incomplete or inconsistent information, and there was a lot of rework (and expensive retesting) when missing information was discovered. They changed the workflow so that the client-oriented teams participated in defining the tests for the work of data clean-up teams. Their tests included sample reports with key relevant data, so the entire pipeline would be aware of what the reports needed to include.

Key benefits

The key advantage of shared test ownership of cross-team boundaries is that both sides have clear expectations of what's inside the shared module. The client team does not need to understand all the internals, of course. Participating in test writing and maintenance gives client teams a solid understanding of the nature and limitations of a critical component they use. The upstream team gets better visibility of the needs of client teams. When tests capture critical client usage scenarios, upstream teams can reduce the possibility of incompatible changes. In general, shared test writing leads to far fewer surprises at both ends.

Another key benefit of shared test writing is that such tests often become good examples of how to use integration points. This reduces the need for upstream teams to maintain and provide separate API documentation for client teams.

The third advantage of joint work is that irrelevant use cases and incomplete solutions are discovered early on. If the client teams can participate in defining tests for integration points, it's far less likely that critical dependencies are missed in implementation.

How to make it work

One of the biggest questions for shared tests, especially in larger companies, is who is ultimately responsible for fixing a failing test. Ideally, the person who introduced the breaking change should spot and fix it immediately, regardless of the team they belong to. Unfortunately, with cross-team boundaries, the change that causes a test to break might not be detected quickly, or even by the person who made that change. As much as possible, try to provide to the upstream team the ability to execute all the shared tests on their own. This might require installing client components on their testing system, or providing access to the test environments of other teams. Allow them to get rapid feedback on whether they've broken a dependent component or not.

Of course, the situation isn't always that simple. If a single upstream team has dozens or hundreds of client teams, it's not going to be economically viable to cater for all dependent components. If you are working in a more complex environment and want to try shared test ideas, check out Eric Evans' book *Domain Driven Design*. In it, Evans presents several good strategies and cross-team patterns for organising work in larger companies – in particular, see the parts of the book that cover context mapping.

AVOID ORGANISING TESTS BY WORK ITEMS

After moving to an iterative delivery model, many teams end up organising their tests along the same lines as their work items. Tests resulting from a user story discussion are grouped and attached to that story, while tests for the next story end up in a different bucket. Often these are stored in the story wiki page or recorded as subtasks of the story in a task management system. This system works reasonably well for the first few months, and then falls apart.

The problem with this approach is that teams practising iterative delivery tend to rewrite, extend and revisit old functionality frequently. As features are extended, reduced or changed, tests for those features have to follow. Coming up with new tests for slightly changed features all the time is not really productive, so test specifications get copied over from previous work items and merged together. But work items and features are not really aligned in iterative delivery. One user story can require changes to several features, and a single feature might be delivered through dozens of stories. This causes friction that does not show up at first, but bites really badly a few months in.

At the start of a process change, copying and merging all the relevant items is easy because there is not a lot of material to analyse. A few months later, that work becomes laborious and error-prone. The more work items are completed, the more difficult it becomes to discover all the relevant parts. Similarly, protecting against unforeseen impacts and functional regression isn't such a big deal early on, but several months into a project it becomes critical for delivery at sustainable pace. Yet, when tests are organised by work items that can extend or cancel the effects of previous work items, it becomes increasingly difficult to know which tests

are still relevant, and which need to be thrown away. Small iterative changes often impact only parts of previous tests, so even when some parts of a test are no longer relevant, other parts may be.

As a software system grows iteratively, so does its set of associated tests, and at some point delivery teams need to trade off speed of feedback against comprehensiveness. This means that someone will need to decide which tests run after each change, which can be executed overnight and which only need to be done occasionally. These decisions are particularly important if teams work with a mix of automated and manual tests. When tests are organised along the lines of work items for delivery, it's impossible for business stakeholders to decide on relative risk or importance of tests. Prioritising tests is often left to delivery teams, or even testers within those teams. This really should be a business risk decision, not a technical one.

If you're just starting to reorganise your process towards a more iterative model, avoid the temptation to group and organise tests along the same lines as your work breakdown. Invest a bit more effort in coming up with a better organisation, and you'll save a lot of time in the future. It's often better to align tests with business processes, because iterative changes tend to introduce a series of small cross-cutting improvements.

Key benefits

When the tests are organised according to business activities, small business changes introduce small organisational changes for tests. This means that tests are easier to maintain. Stakeholders often identify which parts of user activities or business processes need to change, so it is easy to also identify which tests need to be revisited and discussed. Organising tests around business activities also helps to identify duplicates, which is especially important if several teams are working on the same piece of software. When the tests are organised along individual work items, it's impossible for teams to discover small inconsistencies and duplicated work.

Lastly, it's much easier to keep track of the big picture and prioritise testing activities when tests are structured along business activities. It's much easier to engage business stakeholders in the discussion on what needs to be bullet-proof, where we need the fastest feedback, and which tests can be done only occasionally.

How to make it work

A good structure should allow you to quickly discover the full picture for a particular capability or feature, and be easy to extend as new changes come in. Some typical ways of organising tests that work well are by business areas and user work-flows, by feature sets, or even by technical components (such as user interface screens). Different approaches work in different contexts, so it's best to experiment with several ways of organising tests early on.

For consumer software, structuring tests around key user activities is often a good idea. For back-office enterprise software, structure tests around key work-flows or use cases. For automated transaction processing, align tests with transaction types. It will take a bit of time to organise the tests well at the outset, but this time will easily be saved later on.

It's often useful to identify some initial testing ideas for work tasks as a starting point for team discussions. That's how some early examples, screenshots and notes and up in a task management tool. This is perfectly fine, because it helps with the discussions. But that information should not stay in the task management tool after story discussions, otherwise it will lead to tests organised around work items instead of being aligned to business processes.

Once a user story discussion is over and a team accepts the story into delivery, move all associated examples and tests out of the task management tool, merge them with the results of the story discussion and re organise them in line with the testing hierarchy.

Some teams duplicate tests, so they have one copy of a test in the task management tool, and one copy in a testing tool. A common argument for keeping tests in multiple places is to be able to identify a small subset of tests to execute once a story is done, or to have an audit trail of testing changes. However, it's better to provide audit trails with tags and references than having multiple copies. Most test management tools have some way of tagging or marking individual scenarios – use tags to connect user stories to tests and identify small subsets to execute. Multiple sources of truth quickly diverge, and it's better to avoid that.

VERSION CONTROL TESTS ALONG WITH SOFTWARE

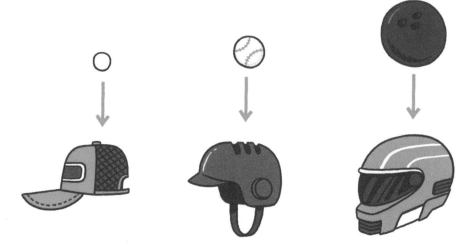

There are plenty of good test management and automation tools today. It's common for teams to use many such tools on the same product for different purposes. That's quite justifiable. However, it also creates a traceability problem, because different tools often store tests in different ways. Some use their own database, some use a shared file system, some keep tests in wiki sites. Keeping tests in many different storage systems makes it difficult to track a relationship between tests and source code versions and branches, especially with a high frequency of change.

Such a setup either introduces instability into tests or delays feedback unnecessarily. If a test is modified before developers start working on a feature change, it will fail until the work is done. This means that the test is useless for checking for regression failures for unrelated changes, and other teams can't use it to check inter-component problems. If a test is not modified before a related software change, then the delivery team working on the change cannot benefit from test-driven development. Testing activities are often delayed until after all software changes are finished, introducing a further feedback delay and separating testing from

development. Some teams work around this by creating copies of tests for in-progress tasks, but this creates unnecessary duplication and only works if there is a single active branch of development. With multiple active versions or branches, it becomes too laborious and error-prone.

Working on multiple branches often requires individual branch configuration parameters. Teams have to capture special configuration values or small execution differences as notes and comments in tests. This makes it impossible to run such tests automatically, so people end up manually executing checks that should really be delegated to a machine. Such an approach often leads to an expectation that lots of tests will fail temporarily on a particular branch, which can mask serious problems until everything comes together. It's also impossible to test an older version if needed, for example to confirm that a hot fix to the production version did not introduce any other regression failures.

On more complex products, the overhead of test management becomes so high that it prevents frequent change. This is especially painful for regulated industries where it is important to prove test traceability. We've worked with several teams where developers were technically capable of working in one-week or two-week iterations and the business analysts were able to support that kind of a cycle, but the prohibitively high cost of test management meant that the teams had to work in quarterly cycles.

Although using multiple testing tools is often blamed for these delays, that's not the key problem. The issue is caused by storing tests outside the main version control system, and that can happen even with a single testing tool. The more complex the underlying product, the more difficult it is to know which version of which test is related to a particular version of the source code. In more complex organisations, several people from different teams might need to work on modifying the same feature, but tests stored outside the main version control effectively prevent such work from happening in parallel.

Rather than enforcing the use of a single test tool, and preventing people from choosing the best tool for a particular job, try to keep all tests in the same version control system as the underlying software code.

Key benefits

When tests and source code are in the same version control system, tests just follow the code whenever a new branch is created, or when two branches are merged back together. It becomes trivial to decide which version of a test is relevant for which version of the code, so teams can truly benefit from test-first development approaches.

Because it becomes easy to test multiple branches, teams can work at a much faster pace. If a bug needs to be hot-fixed in the production version, it's easy to roll back to the appropriate version of tests even if they were changed for the current batch of work. Because version control systems automatically flag potential conflicts, it becomes possible to parallelise work on the same area of code, and split it across different teams. Configuration and environment differences can be captured directly in the tests, which allows teams to safely automate branch-specific tests and avoid false failures caused by incorrect configuration.

Finally, for organisations where test traceability is important, it becomes trivial to prove who changed a test, when and why. That's the entire purpose of version control systems – traceability comes out of the box.

How to make it work

Most testing tools can store or load tests from an external file resource. If you're using such a tool, just make sure that those resources are linked to your main version control system. Avoid binary databases if possible, because they are difficult to merge automatically.

If a tool uses a binary database, but supports automatic import and export from text files, it's often useful to set up automated jobs on a build server to synchronise the test database with an external file system. The exported text source can then be easily kept in a version control system. This at least makes it easy to argue about individual versions, even if changing the active set of tests in the binary database is not fully automated.

If all else fails, keep the entire database as a file in the version control system, and manage conflicts manually. Even tools that use custom databases often support exporting the entire contents of the database as text files, allowing people to merge different versions manually if needed.

CREATE A GALLERY OF EXAMPLES FOR AUTOMATION PATTERNS

When writing tests, people often have to choose between removing duplication and improving readability. In general, it's much more important to make tests easier to read than to ensure that each task is handled by only one piece of test code. Having said that, duplication in test code is one of the most common causes of maintenance problems with test suites.

This problem is particularly common with larger systems, especially when they go through legacy migration projects. In such projects, several different groups of people often need to achieve similar things, but different groups tend to approach tasks slightly differently. Test automation systems built by such groups often contain four or five different ways of achieving the same thing. Over the period of a few months, those approaches start to interleave, which leads to a lot of technical problems and confusion.

We worked with a financial trading fund in London that provided a great example of such problems. Most of their work involved middle-office trade processing, so the majority of tests started with trades coming into the system from an external source. One team automated trade entry using XML messages, another did it directly against Java services. The third team read files with template parameters, and the fourth cloned trades in the database. Each of these approaches, of course, had slightly different names for certain fields. In the XML format, the primary currency of a transaction was marked as PRIMARY_CURRENCY. In the database test automation, it was CURRENCY_1. The XML format was hierarchical, so many concepts were specified using a dot as a hierarchy separator. Counter-parties were specified using CTRPARTY.CODE. The team that used plain text files ignored hierarchical concepts, and invented their own shortcuts for such cases, locating the counter-party records by internal identifiers. Because the developers tried to make each of the automation approaches relatively generic, their code ignored unknown field names instead of reporting them as automation exceptions. This made it almost impossible for people to write correct specifications without constantly peeking below the cover to discover the right naming conventions. Problems with wrong field names were notoriously difficult to troubleshoot. In this case, four different automation approaches didn't actually provide any particular benefit, they were just a product of uncoordinated work. We replaced all those ways of describing trades with a single unified approach that was well documented and used a consistent naming system that was easy to guess. All the various teams could then extend the specifications more easily. When one person improved the automation support for some new trading feature, all the teams could benefit immediately.

The key success factor for creating a single way of entering trades was that we supplied a reference set of examples that showed how to set up different aspects of a trade. These examples didn't actually test anything useful, they just demonstrated how to use automation components. This allowed us to keep them simple and focus on illustrating how to automate things and not get caught up in the complexity of the domain. We called the examples a 'gallery of automation patterns'. The gallery of examples served both as documentation to help new team members understand how to write good checks, but also as a database that anyone could quickly search to see if a feature was already supported or not. This ensured that people would not add ten different ways of doing the same thing unnecessarily in the future.

If you're dealing with a complex system, there is probably a risk of different people automating the same thing in different ways just because it's difficult to find the right information. Consider creating a gallery of automation examples for key aspects of your tests, and make the examples easily accessible.

Key benefits

A gallery of good automation examples makes it easier for people to discover how to get started with test scenarios, which will help to reduce unjustified duplication. This gallery can serve as a central resource of automation patterns, and help to promote a common domain model language in discussions. This will help to build up shared understanding, and make it easier for more people to work on the same software.

How to make it work

It's often useful to create a completely separate hierarchy in the test management tool to hold these examples, because they don't necessarily check anything useful, so they do not need to run with the real tests.

Make sure that the common examples are easy to search and discoverable with only a few clicks. Unless examples are readily accessible, people won't bother checking if something is already implemented before hacking in their own changes.

Finally, don't use a common gallery of examples as an excuse to enforce consistency where it is not appropriate. The fact that you have published automation patterns doesn't mean that all the specifications necessarily need to use them. There are always specific scenarios that might be better served by a different approach, because it might significantly improve readability or isolation. In particular, avoid using components that force you to obscure the purpose of a test in favour of the mechanics of test execution. (See the section *Describe what, not how*) for more information.

DECOUPLE COVERAGE FROM PURPOSE

Because people mix up terminology from several currently popular processes and trends in the industry, many teams confuse the purpose of a test with its area of coverage. They write tests that are slower than they need to be, more difficult to maintain, and often report failures at a much broader level than they need to.

For example, integration tests are often equated with end-to-end testing. In order to check if a service component is talking to the database layer correctly, teams often write monstrous end-to-end tests requiring a dedicated environment, executing workflows that involve many other components. But because such tests are very broad and slow, in order to keep execution time relatively short, teams can afford to exercise only a subset of various communication scenarios between the two components they are really interested in. Instead, it would be much more effective to check the integration of the two components by writing more focused tests. Such tests would directly exercise only the communication scenarios between the two interesting areas of the system, without the rest.

Another classic example of this confusion is equating unit tests with technical checks. This leads to business-oriented checks being executed at a much broader level than they need to be. For example, a team we worked with insisted on running transaction tax calculation tests through their user interface, although the entire tax calculation functionality was localised to a single unit of code. They were misled by thinking about unit tests as developer-oriented technical tests, and tax calculation clearly fell outside of that. Given that most of the risk for wrong tax calculations was in a single Java function, decoupling coverage (unit) from purpose (business test) enabled them to realise that a business-oriented unit test would do the job much better. They rewrote the automation layer for that test and it executed faster and it was a lot cheaper to maintain.

A third common way of confusing coverage and purpose is thinking that acceptance tests need to be executed at a service or API layer. This is mostly driven by a misunderstanding of Mike Cohn's test automation pyramid. In 2009, Cohn wrote an article titled *The Forgotten Layer of the Test Automation Pyramid*, pointing out the distinction between user interface tests, service-level and unit tests. Search for 'test automation pyramid' on Google Images, and you'll find plenty of examples where the middle tier is no longer about API-level tests, but about acceptance tests (the top and bottom are still GUI and unit). Some variants introduce additional levels, such as workflow tests, further confusing the whole picture.

To add insult to injury, many teams try to clearly separate unit tests from what they call 'functional tests' that need different tools. This makes teams avoid unit-testing tools for functional testing, instead introducing horrible monstrosities that run slowly, require record-and-replay test design and are generally automated with bespoke scripting languages that are primitive compared to any modern programming tool.

To avoid this pitfall, make the effort to consider an area of coverage separately from the purpose of a test. Then you're free to combine them. For example, you can have business-oriented unit tests, or technical end-to-end checks.

Key benefits

Thinking about coverage and purpose as two separate dimensions helps teams reduce duplication between different groups of tests, and leads to more focused, faster automation. In addition to speeding up feedback, such focused tests are less brittle, so they will cause fewer false alarms. By speeding up individual test execution, teams can then afford to execute more tests and run them more frequently.

By thinking about technical tests separately from whether they are unit-level, component level or end-to-end tests, teams can also make better decisions on how and where to automate such tests. This often leads to technical tests being written with tools developers that are already familiar with, and helps teams maintain automated tests more easily.

How to make it work

Decide on purpose first, and let the purpose drive the choice of the format in which you capture the test. Business-oriented tests should be written in a language and format that allows teams to discuss potential problems with business domain experts. Technical checks can be written with a technical tool.

Once you've decided on the format and the purpose, think about the minimal area of coverage that would serve the purpose for that particular test. This will mostly be driven by the design of the underlying system. Don't force a test to execute through the user interface just because it's business oriented. If the entire risk for tax calculation is in a single unit of code, by all means write a unit test for it. If the risk is mostly in communication between two components, write a small, focused integration test involving those two areas only.

It's perfectly fine to use tools commonly known as acceptance testing frameworks for writing business-oriented unit tests. They will run faster and be more focused than with a large area of coverage.

Likewise, it's perfectly fine to use tools commonly known as unit testing frameworks for more than just unit tests, as long as such groups of tests are clearly separated so they can be managed and executed individually. If the programmers on the team already know how to use JUnit, for example, it's best to write technical integration tests with this tool, and just execute them with a separate task. In this case, the team can leverage their existing knowledge of a tool for a slightly different purpose.

Beware though of mixing up tests with different areas of coverage, because it becomes impossible to run individual groups in isolation. For example, split out tests into separate libraries so you can run true unit tests in isolation.

AVOID HAVING STRICT COVERAGE TARGETS

Many teams have strict test coverage targets, but they rarely benefit from them. Quite the contrary, coverage targets seem to be the worst of all the blindfolds that teams put on to unknowingly mislead and confuse themselves as they do their testing. Testing is never finished, it's only stopped at some point. Coverage targets offer a convenient stopping point, which is seemingly objective and easy to measure. Unfortunately, they aren't particularly good for that purpose.

Test coverage is a negative metric – it measures how bad something is, not how good it is. Such metrics are great for diagnostic purposes, troubleshooting a particular problem or signalling about potential trouble ahead. Essentially, a very low test coverage figure is a useful piece of information, because it tells us that testing was not performed on part of the product. A very high test coverage figure isn't a particularly useful piece of information, because it doesn't say anything about the type of testing that was performed, or its outcome. So using this metric in isolation is not really productive. In fact, it's often worse than not having a target at all.

Using a negative metric as a target often leads to people gaming the system. For example, a team we worked with was required to meet coverage targets mandated by a new chief information officer initiative. Some parts of their software were thoroughly tested with unit tests, but a major piece of infrastructure code was environment-dependent and had no associated unit tests. The risk, after all, wasn't in a particular unit of code misbehaving, but in the underlying infrastructure changing due to outside influences. As the team had to meet the coverage target globally, they first started writing tests that executed end-to-end integration checks. But they soon decided that such tests were too tedious to maintain, too difficult to write, and too slow to execute. The tests were quickly rewritten to simulate the real environment, use in-memory databases and avoid any external dependencies that would slow down feedback. The team now met the coverage targets, and got a lot of false confidence from the tests executing quickly. Unfortunately, the tests did not really catch any of the big risks – third party libraries changing without anyone noticing, backwards-incompatible messaging formats being introduced by other teams and outside influences on database structures. This is not an isolated example. It's almost impossible to meet arbitrary global coverage targets without writing fake tests that do not check anything, but just improve coverage figures. This is particularly problematic for the areas where the risk is mostly with third-party components outside the control of the team. In many cases the people who write such tests know the metrics aren't reliable, but other people don't and think that something is actually being achieved.

This problem is compounded by the fact that there is no single dimension of coverage that's always useful. There are plenty of ways of measuring the coverage of a software system, such as lines of source code, user interface elements, paths through a workflow, error conditions and so on. Naively measuring only one dimension can provide a lot of unjustified confidence. For example, proving that 99% of the code has been well tested might sound good, but what if one of the key user flows is completely in the remaining 1%?

Avoid having strict global targets for coverage if possible. Instead, use coverage as an internal diagnostic metric – a signal of where you might need to improve testing activities.

Key benefits

When coverage metrics are used only for internal diagnostics, and not as a generic target, teams need to find more meaningful metrics to explain when they've done enough testing. This makes people engage better with stakeholders to define acceptable risk levels and different measurements of quality.

Without a misleading target that's easy to measure, teams are less likely to be blinded by the false confidence provided by coverage metrics, or sucked into tunnel vision, focusing too much on a single dimension of coverage.

How to make it work

Above all, don't use coverage metrics in isolation as a signal that something is good, complete or thoroughly tested. Try to avoid publishing coverage metrics outside the team, as they are likely to be misused for setting targets or cross-team comparisons that don't make any sense.

If you absolutely have to declare a coverage target publicly, at least reduce the risk of tunnel vision setting in by using several dimensions of coverage. For example, set targets for code coverage, path coverage and user activity coverage. For some useful inspiration about this, see Lee Copeland's book *A Practitioner's Guide to Software Test Design*. In it, he discusses the following potential levels of coverage:

1. statements (lines of code)
2. decisions (conditional execution branches)
3. conditions (causes of selecting branches)
4. combinations of conditions and decisions
5. combinations of multiple conditions
6. executing loops multiple times
7. paths through the system

Coverage targets only work in combination with other insights. In the cases where we've seen them actually work well, they were always combined with human intelligence. In particular, coverage metrics tend to work well for clearly scoped exploratory testing sessions. In such cases, though, coverage is almost always measured against cross-cutting concerns, such as key risks, user activities or capabilities, not against lines of code or software features.

MEASURE YOUR TESTS' HALF-LIFE

The vast majority of teams we meet these days have embraced test automation, often using tools that allow the easy extension and addition of tests. This can result in the rapid creation of large numbers of tests. Each and every one of those tests requires maintenance to ensure they are still valuable, up-to-date and keep passing. Over time this can become a significant ownership investment, yet few teams formally check the cost of maintenance, or whether it is money well spent.

Start measuring the half-life of your tests, that is, their stability. Practically this means measuring the amount of change within your tests and their associated underlying features.

Use this data as an input to trigger analysis into why they are changing that much and whether a course of action is needed to address them. For example, if the data points to brittle, intermittently failing, and poorly written tests then maybe some investment is needed to refactor or rewrite the tests to make them more reliable. Alternatively, it might indicate that a part of the system is more prone to bugs, requiring increased testing, both automated and exploratory.

Key benefits

Having a measure of the stability of tests gives teams some really useful information with which to inspect and adapt their testing strategy. This information can guide decisions on where to invest more or less time in testing.

Instability gives an indication about areas of the system that might be riskier and require further, more concentrated, testing. If an area of the system is critical to the business yet is covered by tests that are frequently changing (and quite possibly people are not aware), then knowledge of this could indicate a need to bolster coverage. Failing automated tests, that are immediately fixed without any deeper analysis, may mean that areas of weakness in the system are not identified quickly enough (or even at all). It's much better to identify these weaknesses by analysing tests than in production.

Tests that need to be frequently updated because they intermittently fail point to a potential problem with test design, or maybe even fragility in the underlying system. Maybe the test automation should be implemented in a different way, for example, using blocking for a specific event to happen rather than waiting for a period of time.

How to make it work

Establish a reliable way of measuring the rate of change of tests. Typically we've seen this done by measuring the number of check-ins for each test. This requires storing tests in a version control system. When you measure the number of changes and the interval between changes, you start to notice those tests that need the most maintenance. Also, why not measure how many bugs get found by each test or feature. One idea is to create a heat map showing the amount of change in tests and/or failing tests grouped by business feature. That is a nice way to highlight areas to investigate further.

Our expectation is that tests tend to have a shorter half-life early on, changing quite regularly as the parts of the system they are covering also evolve. But after these features become a stable part of the product, the related tests should not change as much, neither

should we expect to continue finding many genuine test failures (and therefore defects) in these areas.

Analysing the reasons for instability in tests gives useful feedback. Typically we've found the feedback points to one of three main underlying reasons:

- A volatile or evolving part of the system, often involving continued new feature requests, meaning new development and probably a fair amount of refactoring too.
- A weaker part of the solution where more bugs are detected, possibly a part central to the design that is regularly changed or impacted by the addition of new features.
- The tests are fragile and need to be refactored

Analyse the areas of greatest change and consider what is causing the instability, then decide on a course of action. You might decide to raise technical improvement work items to change the test suite or the system under test. Some teams adopt a strategy to improve a weaker part of the test suite when they are making changes in that area and do this continuously based on the half-life analysis.

In some cases, this information has led to a wholesale change in the way that test automation is implemented. An example we've seen repeatedly is where a team stops using a user interface automation framework, because of the fragility and high cost of maintaining the tests when this part of the system is frequently changed.

Instead of quarantining flickering tests, performing this analysis may point to a pattern of weakness or failure across tests that can be resolved by a change in the common automation code they share.

OPTIMISE FOR READING, NOT WRITING

Due to a combination of focus on productivity and creative salesmanship, the speed of writing tests seems to play an undeservedly important role today. Focusing too much on how quickly tests are written leads to an instant sense of achievement but a horrible waste of time later on.

For example, we worked with a team at an insurance company that hired a third-party consultancy to write tests for a critical piece of their calculation engine. The management thought that the developers were too expensive to write the tests, and the testers were too busy. They chose a company that promised to write a lot of tests quickly, and it was encouraged to speed things up because it was paid by time. Six months later, the insurance company was worse off than if it had no tests. Out of a thousand or so tests that the consultants had delivered, more than half were failing. Developers completely ignored the tests, because they were unreliable. The testers tried to fix them, but ultimately they couldn't keep pace with development, so the whole effort had just been a waste of time.

This isn't a problem just with third-party consultants ripping people off. The most popular commercial test automation tools today tend to be sold on how quickly they help people knock up tests. There is a lot of emphasis on easy test creation, reusing parts of tests and generic support for testing almost anything. This is great for sales, but unfortunately exactly the wrong thing for long-term test maintenance.

In order to make tests easy to write for any platform, such tools tend to require generic interfaces and generic controls. They make people describe tests in the language of the user interface instead of the language of the underlying business domain. This trade-off brings great ease of creation when someone has a clear idea of what they want a test to do, but it does not communicate the purpose, and does not transfer the knowledge with the test. Other people won't be able to understand the test easily. When the test catches a problem in the future, it won't be easy to discover what failed. When such tests need to change, it is very difficult to pinpoint the places that need to be rewritten. Ironically, such tests are typically tied to the user interface, which is often the part that changes the most. The false sense of productivity generated when 700 tests get quickly written disappears when people need to maintain those tests. Small changes in user interface can break large numbers of tests, and because they are difficult to analyse, often the only option is to rewrite everything from scratch. Tools that help to write tests quickly keep people very busy, but not really productive.

There are just two moments when an automated test provides useful information: the first time it passes and when it subsequently fails. Before a test passes for the first time, the functionality required by it is not yet there. The first green bar on a test should reliably tell us that the feature is now there, and that it does what we want it to do. Subsequent test passes don't really require attention or action – when a test is passing nobody needs to do anything. The next time someone actually makes a decision based on the test is when it fails. At that point, it is telling us that we broke something, or that there is an unplanned impact on a related piece of software. In both these situations, tests optimised for writing totally fail to be of use.

If a test is not easy to understand, it's difficult to argue about completeness, so we won't be able to know for sure that our work is done when it passes for the first time. Similarly, if a test is difficult to understand, and doesn't clearly communicate its purpose, pinpointing problems is very difficult when it fails.

It's far better to optimise tests for reading than for writing. Spending half an hour more writing a test will save days of investigation later on. Avoid using tools that allow people to knock up dozens of tests quickly, because such tests won't be easy to maintain or understand.

Key benefits

Tests that are easy to understand will be easier to update and maintain. It's much easier to know whether the work is done or not when they pass, and it's much faster to diagnose and discover problems when they fail. However, improved readability of tests brings benefits far beyond just catching problems. Tests are often the most accurate documentation about a system. New people joining teams can quickly get up to speed by reading the tests. People can use tests for discussions about potential changes.

How to make it work

Tailor the format, the language and the concepts used in a test to the primary reading audience. When a test is for a business rule or a business process, write it so that people who performing that process can understand it. Write technical tests so that developers can find their way around them quickly. Use the language of the user interface only when describing tests that need to be read by user interface designers. Then choose tools that allow you to automate tests written in those ways.

In business-oriented tests, if you need to compromise either ease of maintenance or readability, keep readability. Duplication of parts of tests is a typical example. Programmers are trained professionally to fight against duplication, so they extract similar parts into common components so that they can change them in a single place. In business-oriented tests, having each test spell out the relevant inputs and outputs makes them easier to understand in isolation. In particular, avoid reusing technical automation components just because they do something similar to what you need. It's far better to describe each test separately so it can be easily understood.

NAME TESTS FOR SEARCH ENGINE OPTIMISATION

Test names (and scenario names) rarely get the attention they deserve. Test names are mostly generic, such as 'payroll acceptance test' or 'negative path scenario'. It seems as if most tests have names purely because file systems require files to be named, or because a wiki needs a unique URL for each page.

Generic test names make it incredibly difficult to identify existing tests that correspond to proposed feature changes. This significantly increases the maintenance costs of larger systems. For example, if we're working on adding multi-currency support to payments, and the payments module has a hundred generically named tests, it's unlikely that anyone will spend time trying to understand which of the existing tests should be modified to capture the new features. It's much more likely that people will just add another test. This leads to a lot of duplication, which is difficult to identify and manage, increasing the cost of future test maintenance. Adding new tests for every change is a vicious circle, because it becomes even more difficult

to understand what existing tests cover, so the problem just gets bigger over time.

Generic names are a wasted opportunity to provide a navigation guide through a large test suite. Because there is no easy way to discover relevant tests for a feature, testers and developers have to read the contents of individual scenarios to understand potential changes. This process is time-consuming and error-prone.

Likewise, when a test fails, the name of the scenario or the feature is the first piece of information teams get from the test runner. Generic names can be misleading, and require developers to find and understand the contents of a test in order to determine whether the failure is an unforeseen impact, an expected change or indicates a bug.

Good test names are specific, and they pinpoint the purpose of the test or the scenario. Think of test names as keywords for quick discovery. Imagine that the test was an online document and that you were looking for it using a search engine. Capture the keywords you would use to search for it, and turn them into the title. Apply all the search engine optimisation tricks you know to create a good name. Avoid generic words and broad statements. Remove all words that do not relate to its purpose.

For example, in 'simple acceptance test for payroll', the first four words are completely generic, and could apply to pretty much anything, so they are useless. 'Payroll' is the only word that matters, but since payroll is probably handled by a software module that has hundreds of associated tests, the test name does not tell us anything. More specific names such as 'payroll net salary calculation', or 'payroll tax deductions' would achieve much more.

Key benefits

Good names are crucial for managing larger sets of tests or scenarios, because they allow teams to quickly identify all tests or scenarios related to a particular feature. Business analysts can discover all relevant tests and use them as a starting point for impact analysis. Testers can identify interesting boundaries and edge cases when designing checks for similar features. Developers can identify subsets of tests to execute in order to check quickly that new code does not introduce any regression failures.

Specific names help us to spot whether a test is trying to do too much and avoid bloat. They help us to spot if a test scenario should be extended, or if a completely different scenario needs to be added for some new functionality. This helps to avoid duplication and uncontrollable growth of test suites over time.

If a failing test has a name that explains its specific purpose, developers might be able to understand what went wrong even without looking at its contents. This can significantly speed up troubleshooting and fixing complex systems with large numbers of tests.

How to make it work

A good heuristic for naming tests is to imagine a hierarchical navigation through the test suite, then collect all the names of the modules that would lead to a particular test. Add to that name whatever makes a particular test specific or different from the other tests in the same group. For example, tests describing net salary calculations in payroll could be named 'Payroll – calculations – net salary – full-time employees' and 'Payroll – calculations – net salary – part-time employees'. Most test management tools allow you to group tests and suites into hierarchies, so this kind of naming can become the foundation for a good hierarchical structure.

Avoid using conjunctions (and, or, not) in test names. Conjunctions are a sign the test is trying to do too much, or lacks focus. At the XP Day 2009 conference in London, Mark Striebeck spoke about an analysis of tests at Google where they evaluated whether a test was good or not based on what happened when it failed. If the code was changed or added to after a failure to resolve the problem, the test was marked as good. If people changed the test to make it pass, it was marked as bad. Conjunctions in test names were one of the clear patterns that emerged in the second category. A conjunction suggests that a single test is trying to check several things, which makes it more brittle and difficult to maintain. See the section *One test, one topic* for some information on how to restructure such tests.

EXPLAIN THE PURPOSE OF A TEST IN THE INTRODUCTION

Lack of context is one of the root causes of major maintenance problems with large test suites. A machine can execute a test without knowing why it needs to do it, and push around bits of data provided by the test specification, but the absence of a good context makes it impossible for humans to change test data in the future. This problem is not really visible when someone writes a test, because they have enough context in their heads to evaluate and understand the bits and pieces passed in and out by the test. However, a few months later, that understanding will be gone.

Because contextual information is not really needed at the time when a test is written, tests rarely have any good introductory information. Even when the automation tool requires some header text, people often do not give this enough thought. They often specify the context too broadly, talking about entire subsystems or components. Contextual descriptions are often forced into a standardised template, frequently in the form of a user story, but this is too broad and often incomplete or misleading. One of the teams we worked with recently had all their Cucumber specifications written so that they started 'As an admin, because I want to manage the system, I want ... feature'. The first two parts of that sentence are generic and appeared in all the tests, making them utterly irrelevant for understanding any particular test. The third part just named the technical feature that the test was related to, which could be inferred from the file name as well. Something was written as a context in each file, but it was a complete waste of time. Even worse, it was a wasted opportunity to make the tests understandable in the future.

Another common misuse of context in tests is to explain the mechanics of test execution. In the case of automated tests, this is pretty much a waste of time.

The correct definition of how a test is executed is in the automation layer, and any textual descriptions are likely to get out of date as the system evolves.

As a result of all this, an explanation of the purpose of a test is rarely available to anyone who was not present at the time the test was written. The more time passes, the bigger the ensuing problems.

Instead of jumping over the context too quickly, try explaining why you've chosen a particular set of examples, and why this particular test is actually important. Answer the question 'why?' in the context, and let the rest of the test deal with 'what' and 'how'.

Key benefits

Good context at the start of a test is crucial to avoid information bottlenecks in the future. Without context, only the person who actually wrote a test will know what needs to change in response to system changes, and that person might not even be around over longer time periods. Contextual information explaining why something was written in the first place enables anyone to evaluate at a later date whether a test is still needed, to identify the right people to speak to if some values need to change, and to spot potential functional gaps and inconsistencies as they extend the system. Unless all your colleagues have perfect memory, all this information is helpful even to the person who wrote a particular test.

Contextual information enables teams to discuss the tests more effectively with external stakeholders. Decision makers will need to know the purpose of a test and why certain examples were chosen to critique and validate test scenarios. Such people rarely participate in writing tests, and without a purpose-oriented context they will not be able to provide good feedback.

How to make it work

A quick way of discovering what needs to be explained in the context is to show a test to someone new, and try to explain it. That person shouldn't be someone completely outside the domain – don't show it to a random passer-by on your street, because that's not the target audience for your test. A good test subject is someone who works for the same company as you but not in your team. That person should have a good amount of domain expertise and broadly know what you're talking about, but they would not have participated in the process of designing the test. This is a relevant simulation for a new colleague, or someone else from your team reading the test six months in the future. Pay attention to how you're explaining the test, and consider that pretty much anything you say should go into the context. This ensures that the document can be understood without you. Otherwise, you will have to repeat the same process over and over again with different people in the future.

An alternative approach is to show the test to someone and keep quiet, letting the reader ask questions. The answers to their questions are a good starting point for the context.

Avoid repeating the data or the information already provided by the body of the test. Instead, explain why you've chosen those particular examples, or that particular way of specifying the test.

Also avoid one-sentence templates. Those are too generic to be useful. In particular, avoid trying to force descriptions into the format of a user story. This almost never works well, because tests shouldn't really be structured around work task hierarchies (see the section *Avoid organising tests by work items* for more information on why that is bad).

SPLIT JUST-IN-CASE TESTS FROM KEY EXAMPLES

At a gaming company we worked with a few years ago, there were several types of customer accounts. One was a legacy account migrated from an old call centre system, another was for people who directly registered through the new website, and a third was for people who were referred by a third party. When discussing requirements, business people generally spoke about only one customer type, as they viewed all categories as the same. However, because the information for different customer types was stored in different database tables, with similar but slightly different structures, testers often discovered problems when trying things out using legacy accounts.

When the technical model is misaligned with the business model, the key business examples probably won't cover all the risks properly. The technical model can have its own edge cases and boundary conditions that do not exist in the business model. This is clearly a modelling problem rather than a testing problem, but sometimes there is very little we can do about it. With legacy systems, the underlying model might be too difficult or too expensive to change as new requirements come in. Although ten key examples might capture the developers' shared understanding of a new requirement, testers might be justifiably concerned about many more edge cases.

When the model cannot be changed easily, teams often struggle to manage all the test ideas. If key examples and additional technical tests are bundled together, there is a risk that documents will become too difficult to understand and maintain easily. It also slows down critical feedback on features, because additional examples are checked each time the key examples need to be validated. However, if the two groups of examples are separated, it becomes difficult to identify all the examples that need to be checked for a software change, and people often duplicate work unnecessarily.

A good way to handle this situation is to create a separate document for additional examples and cross-link the two test specifications, but use the same automation. Testers can then reuse automation hooks and fixtures developed for key examples to add loads more tests quickly, and if they find any really significant differences those cases can become key examples for the future.

Key benefits

Having separate specification documents that reuse the same automation allows teams to do assisted exploratory testing and quickly try out lots of different additional scenarios, even keeping them in a regression test suite if needed. At the same time, because the key examples are in a separate document, teams can use them for shared understanding and stakeholder feedback.

The specification with the key examples can be used to get critical feedback quickly, for example developers can ensure that the key examples pass before submitting the change to the version control system, and additional examples can be checked later using a continuous integration server.

Splitting the examples allows teams to create a pipeline of continuous build jobs, so that they can get feedback on failures quickly even if there are hundreds of technical examples. A common set-up is to execute only the key examples using a primary continuous build job, and then run the secondary examples only if the primary job succeeds. With more complex models,

the additional examples can also be split into several different build jobs to optimise feedback. For example, examples from the areas that do not change frequently could be executed overnight instead of after every source code change.

Separate documents also make test maintenance cheaper. If the model changes, and as a consequence tests break, it's generally sensible just to fix the key examples and throw away the additional ones. Keeping the extra examples wouldn't make a lot of sense because the model has changed, so there is probably a completely different set of risks that need to be covered.

How to make it work

With web-based systems such as FitNesse, we generally create an entirely separate hierarchy for additional examples. Cross-links to the extra examples are typically in the footers of the key web pages, with a sentence such as 'For a more complete technical set of checks, see...'. This keeps the key documents short and easy to read. Separate hierarchies ensure that people can't unintentionally start browsing technical cases when they are trying to understand how the system works.

With file-based systems such as Cucumber, cross-linking is a lot more difficult. We tend to keep both groups of examples in the same file, but the key examples are on the top, and there is a clear separation between them and the additional scenarios. People can just stop reading when they get to the technical part. It's also useful to use tags to mark additional examples and scenarios. People can quickly execute only the scenarios without the tag for quick feedback, and continuous build tools can execute additional scenarios as secondary jobs.

LET THE CHAOS MONKEY OUT PERIODICALLY

Technical code coverage is relatively easy to measure, but it doesn't actually say much about the effectiveness of a test system. Risk coverage theoretically gives a much better measurement of effectiveness, but it is also a lot more difficult to measure. The more complex the underlying interactions and components, the more difficult it becomes to argue about key risk coverage, because many moving parts could interfere with test results or distort them. In addition, risk coverage is often measured against a checklist of key risks or some other way of theoretically predicting where the problems can come from, which may or may not match the real situation.

A good set of tests should warn about unexpected impacts and prevent functional regression problems. The best way to check if it will serve that purpose is to actually cause problems and see if the tests catch them.

Netflix is famous for their approach to testing network resilience. They run a service in production (aptly called Chaos Monkey) that randomly switches off virtual machines and causes other types of common network failures, just to ensure that the system can survive similar issues if they arise in real use. Using the same approach, we can make the test system cover business risks more thoroughly, and reduce the possibility that unexpected bugs or impacts are introduced into software without anyone noticing. Look at critical parts of the software, break them and run the tests. If the alarm bells sound, that part of the process is well covered with tests. If nothing happens, it's time to write some more tests.

There are many automated tools that cause changes to software and measure test results – they are often bundled under the category of mutation testing tools.

But don't take this idea as just advice to apply a mutation testing tool. Such utilities introduce technical changes based on technical code analysis, so the impact is mostly technical. The effort involved in producing and testing mutations is often directly correlated with technical complexity. A low-risk complex component might get a lot more attention than a highly critical but very simple module. Instead of using the technical landscape as the primary dimension of change for mutations, try creating your own mutations manually by driving them from a risk model.

Key benefits

Letting the chaos monkey out now and then during testing allows teams to cause artificial crises when it's safe to do so. They can improve their processes without having to put out fires at the same time.

For example, working with an ecommerce system a few years ago, we let the chaos monkey out on the shipping calculator and discovered that it was quite easy to break it without causing any alarms. The shipping calculator didn't often change, but it was enhanced once or twice a year, and this was always a fiddly process. The team had some tests around it, but everyone was surprised how few problems they caught. This allowed us to do a blameless post-mortem, in which we decided how to test the calculator component differently. It also helped to make it clear that the organisation needed to invest a lot more effort in spreading domain knowledge throughout the team, so that more people could get involved in testing shipping rules and resolving production issues if they happened.

Manually deciding on mutations allows people to apply critical thinking and deep domain knowledge to achieve the most risk coverage with fewest mutations,

focusing on business risk and not just technical changes. Trying out difficult and risky mutations provides more confidence in bug prevention capabilities, and it also helps teams to discover important missing test scenarios. These discoveries can then inform exploratory testing sessions to probe further in the same area.

How to make it work

Think of chaos monkey sessions just as a type of exploratory testing activity that requires the involvement of a slightly larger, more cross-functional, group. For the best results, schedule such sessions periodically, time-box them and agree on a list of key risks to explore.

Teams that use an attribute-component-capability matrix to plan testing can repurpose the routes through their ACC matrix for chaos monkey sessions. This has the added benefit of immediately identifying the set of tests that should ideally catch the problem, so you can speed up feedback.

The chaos monkey approach can improve both automated checks and manual exploratory testing processes. When used to improve automated checks, it's easier to focus on one problem at a time and rerun all relevant tests. This can be done with different pairs of developers and testers quickly iterating through different potential problems. When used to improve exploratory testing, it's often better to introduce several problems, deploy a test version of the system, and then let multiple groups explore in parallel and look for the same issues. When the whole team debriefs after the exploratory testing sessions, compare who caught what and discuss the differences in approaches. This will help you improve your exploratory testing practices across the entire group.

BIBLIOGRAPHY

- Domain-Driven Design: Tackling Complexity in the Heart of Software by Eric Evans, ISBN 978-0321125217, Addison-Wesley Professional 2003
- How Google Tests Software by James A. Whittaker, Jason Arbon and Jeff Carollo, ISBN 978-0321803023, Addison-Wesley Professional 2012
- More Agile Testing: Learning Journeys for the Whole Team by Lisa Crispin and Janet Gregory, ISBN 978-0321967053, 978-0321967053
- Lessons Learned in Software Testing: A Context-Driven Approach by by Cem Kaner, James Bach and Bret Pettichord, ISBN 978-0471081128, Wiley 2001
- Explore It!: Reduce Risk and Increase Confidence with Exploratory Testing by Elisabeth Hendrickson, ISBN 978-1937785024, Pragmatic Bookshelf 2013
- A Practitioner's Guide to Software Test Design by Lee Copeland, ISBN 978-1580537919, Artech House 2004
- The Checklist Manifesto: How to Get Things Right by Atul Gawande, ISBN 978-0312430009, Picador 2011
- Simple Testing Can Prevent Most Critical Failures: An Analysis of Production Failures in Distributed Data-Intensive Systems by Ding Yuan, Yu Luo, Xin Zhuang, Guilherme Renna Rodrigues, Xu Zhao, Yongle Zhang, Pranay U. Jain, and Michael Stumm, University of Toronto, from 11th USENIX Symposium on Operating Systems Design and Implementation, ISBN 978-1-931971-16-4, USENIX Association 2014
- User Story Mapping: Discover the Whole Story, Build the Right Product by Jeff Patton, ISBN 978-1491904909, O'Reilly Media 2014

Useful web resources

Access these links quickly at http://www.50quickideas.com

- Fifty Quick Ideas discussion group
  https://groups.google.com/forum/#!forum/50quickideas
- QUPER web site
  http://quper.org
- Chaos Monkey Released Into The Wild, by Ariel Tseitlin 2012
  http://techblog.netflix.com/2012/07/chaos-monkey-released-into-wild.html
- Improving Testing Practices at Google, a conference report on Mark Striebeck's presentation at XPDay 2009
  http://gojko.net/2009/12/07/improving-testing-practices-at-google
- The Forgotten Layer of the Test Automation Pyramid by Mike Cohn, 2009
  http://www.mountaingoatsoftware.com/blog/the-forgotten-layer-of-the-test-automation-pyramid

This book is part of a series of books on improving various aspects of iterative delivery. If you like it, check out the other books from the series at **50quickideas.com**.

FIFTY QUICK IDEAS
TO IMPROVE YOUR
USER
STORIES

by Gojko Adzic and David Evans

FIFTY QUICK IDEAS
TO IMPROVE YOUR
RETRO
SPECTIVES

by Tom Roden and Ben Williams